COMPLETING THE WRITER'S TO-DO LIST

Tonya Price's Fiction

Short Story Collections

Fiction River: Hidden Crime, anthology mystery short story: "Night of the Healer." November 2015

Strange New Worlds III

Strange New Worlds IV

Strange New Worlds V

Short Stories in Fiction River Anthologies

Hard Choices Anthology – Thriller short story, "Payback"

Stolen Anthology – Mystery short story, "Stealing Amy"

Feel the Love Anthology – Romance short story

Spies! Anthology – Thriller short story, "Spy in the Sky"

COMPLETING THE WRITER'S TO-DO LIST

Tonya D. Price

 magnolia
LANE PRESS

Contents

Introduction

Nothing is more stressful than going to sleep and waking up in the middle of the night with the sudden realization you promised an editor you would have a revision to them by the morning that you forgot to start writing.

Today authors are responsible for so many tasks that it has become impossible for even those writers blessed with excellent memories to recall everything they need to do, want to do or have promised they would accomplish during the day. Our inability to keep track of every task we feel we should be doing stems from the fact humans did not evolve to handle our lengthy to-do lists.

In their academic paper, "The Pen is Mightier Than The Keyboard – Advantages of Longhand Over Laptop Note Taking," Pam A. Mueller, and Daniel M. Oppenheimer[1] show that the human brain was not designed to store and retrieve the number of details that modern life demands of us. However, no species on Earth is as adaptive as humans. Our ability to adjust to changing conditions is what has contributed to human survival despite ice ages, droughts, and the emergence of the information age. As the torrent of demands on our time and attention grows, people have devised ways to deal with the amount of data we must process each day.

In 2001, author David Allen released *Getting Things Done: The Art of Stress-free Productivity*[2], a groundbreaking book that revolutionized how business professionals managed the information deluge that they faced. The lessons Allen taught formed the basis of subsequent approaches developed to control the amount of incoming information. In the intervening years, technology has both increased the number of tasks we need to perform and produced a variety of new tools for managing lists. However, due to the fast pace of innovation and adaptation of technology, most of us are left on our own to figure out how to organize our time to complete all the things required of us by our career, family, and leisure activities.

What this book will teach you

Completing the Writer's To-Do List builds on established methodologies such as the one developed by David Allen. In addition, we review subsequent approaches, and discuss the author's own experience to illustrate processes, which may be used to manage the enormous amount of tasks a writer confronts on a daily basis.

Writers find it increasingly difficult to track every requirement of running a writing business. In addition to research and writing a book, indie publishers also produce their work. At a high level, this includes working with a cover designer, copy editor, beta reader, proofreader, and interior layout designer. Indie publishers must also manage their marketing strategy, advertising campaigns, distribution process, and follower relationships. You can probably think of a couple of additional responsibilities not listed.

All too often, motivated writing entrepreneurs spend a weekend organizing their checklist of projects to complete, only to discover a month later they are once again losing track of what work they want to complete. This book will help you understand why this occurs and how to avoid that situation.

Downloads

You can access all downloads for this book from the Business Books for Writer's website at:

www.BusinessBooksForWriters.com/to-do-links

Recommended tools

Throughout the text tools are identified you can use to make it easier to organize and complete your tasks.

One of the tools discussed is Todoist (www.todoist.com). You can sign up for the free version or a premium subscription. Some of the discussions in the following chapters focus on features that are only available in the Todoist paid premium account. To start, get the free version to make sure you are comfortable using the program. Then, after you have been using your new process for completing your to-do list, pay for the premium version if you find yourself wishing you had the additional features.

The features in the premium version of Todoist are mentioned to let readers know the features are available and to point out how to use them since they can save you a lot of time and help you stay more organized.

Learn how to capture your tasks

A methodology will be introduced for gathering your items in one place so you can track your work. In addition, you will discover how to manage your information going forward, and if your life gets complicated and you get behind again, learn how to re-establish control of what you need to accomplish.

Part 1: Gathering the tools you will need

The book is organized into four sections. Part 1 will help you understand why you struggle with staying up-to-date with your tasks and why most people create lists only to abandon them.

After understanding why most people fail to accomplish their goals for the day, we will review the plan for getting your to-do list under control in a weekend. We will then review how to customize a process that works for you. Illness, unexpected opportunities and a variety of other circumstances can cause a build-up of unfinished work. You need a plan for recovering after you have had a setback.

Part 2: Preparing for success

My father once told me that to be a good carpenter you need the right tools. Likewise, success in finishing everything you need to complete each day requires the right tools and knowing how to use them.

You can get various apps, programs, and strategies to help you get things done. You can manage all aspects of your to-do list in a program such as Outlook, but many writers prefer to use programs specifically aimed at collecting their to-dos or storing their completed tasks. We will recommend an approach and then show you how to experiment with other methods so you can tailor your system to the way you like to work.

Never be afraid of adjusting your approach as you learn more about what works for you.

Part 3: Developing a system that works for you

The third part of the book will review a five-stage system for tracking, completing, and maintaining your to-do items from the many sources where they are stored, using the five-stage approach developed by David Allen in his book, *Getting Things Done: The Art of Stress-Free Productivity*.[3]

In Chapter 5 you will learn how to create a process that always captures your to-do items, while Chapter 6 discusses the benefits of using a document management system for archiving your information, so you can find the material you need when you need it.

Part 4: Your process

One reason writers start a to-do list and then never complete the work they need to finish is that they lack a review process for remembering what tasks they want to complete after the first few days. In Chapter 7, you will learn how to set up a system to capture, schedule, and complete your task list.

Your email account(s) play a significant role in your task management system. Email is often the source of your to-do list and can form the basis of your permanent record-keeping system. Chapter 8 discusses how to end each day with zero emails in your Inbox. Cleaning up your daily emails so that you can deal with incoming messages efficiently, leaves you time to complete your work, rather than just moving messages from email folder to email folder. Finishing the day with no emails in your Inbox allows you to feel a sense of accomplishment that your work for the day is done, reducing your stress level.

Chapter 9 talks about what information you need to document and how to store that information for later reference. Filing documents is an easy exercise many writing entrepreneurs put off because there are always more pressing matters to deal with; however, this makes it hard to find information such as tax forms and receipts, when you need them. Making record-keeping part of your to-do list process will allow you to locate this information quickly, providing you with more writing time.

The chapter ends with an acknowledgment that almost everyone who tries to get their to-do list under control encounters difficulties at some point. After reviewing the kinds of situations that might cause you to get behind, strategies are introduced to get you back on track.

The book concludes with a chapter listing resources where you can learn more about developing, following, and maintaining your list. Use these resources to fine tune your task management strategy, and discover tools available to simplify the entire process.

How this book fits in the Business Books for Writers series

Since writers are busy professionals each book in the Business Books for Writers series is short so you can read it in a weekend. *The Writer's Business Plan*[4], helps writing entrepreneurs decide what they want their business to accomplish and what they want to achieve with their company. *Meeting the Writer's Deadline* introduced strategies for completing writing projects by helping writers set clear goals for their writing enterprise and a strategy for achieving those goals.

The current book, as the third in the series, fills in the next step in the process: taking the goals and tasks created by the previous two books and bringing them under your control, thereby allowing you to spend more time writing, making it easier to hit your deadlines and reach your writing business goals.

Help aids

Each of the Business Books for Writers contains examples, checklists, worksheets, and templates, so readers do not have to reinvent these helpful tools. Feel free to modify them as needed for your personal use.

Print readers will find a webpage listing all the URLs in the book that can be used to easily access online resources. For Completing the Writers To-Do List, the URL page is found at:

www.businessbooksforwriters.com/ctwtdl-links

Website resources for this book

You will find a unique web page on the Business Books for Writers website where any corrections to the manuscript found after publication are listed. While we work hard to catch all errors through our professional copyediting, proofreading, and layout stages, a small typo might occasionally occur. You can find the current crop of potential errors with corrections at:

www.businessbooksforwriters.com/book-updates

Additional Information

I received positive comments from readers regarding the tips, hints, and end of chapter review points contained in books one, and two of the series, so look for these throughout the book. Below is your first tip box!

TIP: You need a system

Many writers get frustrated with their inability to complete everything they need to do to run a business. Getting behind becomes a source of stress, and it is not uncommon for writers to start thinking of themselves as a failure. The secret to completing your to-do list is to develop a system. That is what *Completing The Writer's To-Do List* teaches you to do.

Part 1: Creating A Master List

Chapter 1: Gathering The Tools You Will Need

Managing the many tasks that we need to accomplish when running a writing business is a crucial skill for a writer. The job can be overwhelming.

Having a reliable process will help us manage our tasks. In fact, most people quit tracking their obligations because they don't have a system for determining the order in which they should complete their commitments.

Desperate not to get behind in their work as they have before, writers may tackle the issue that seems to be the most important. Starting a new item without reviewing everything that needs to be done allows essential items to linger forgotten at the bottom of our pile. We remember these forgotten tasks when we miss a promised delivery date, fail to pay a bill on time or make our launch date only to discover we forgot to approve the final cover design.

Avoid this situation by developing a process for creating, managing, and maintaining a list of what you need to accomplish. This list can then function as a trusted business tool you can depend on to help grow your business and establish your reputation as a professional writer.

So let's break the old cycle once and for all.

Devote this coming weekend to establishing a system for keeping track of all your tasks, and deciding the order in which you will finish what you want to complete. This book will be your guide.

Expect that at some point you may find you have slipped out of the habit of using your system. Illness, vacations, family emergencies, even incredible opportunities can arise causing writers to abandon their schedule; but when life throws off your plan, do not give up! Instead, get out this book and take the following weekend to go through the steps described and start using your system again. Don't assume because you stop using your system that it wasn't working. Many writers find it takes several attempts before they hit upon the right system that works for them.

1.1 Organizing the process you use

You can manage your work using just an email program. However, as you develop your system, you may find, as many writers do, that multiple approaches reinforce each other and work best.

No matter how you track what you need to get done, remember the simpler the process, the more likely you are to follow it. You want to have an easy way to capture items you need to complete. You also need more than one way to remind yourself what you are going to do each day. You want a reminder system that works when you are away from your computer, or if you don't have your cell phone or a notebook in front of you.

Capturing your to-do list, having a process for evaluating each task you need to finish and scheduling how and when you will complete these tasks is an important habit to develop. Organizing your responsibilities reduces the stress of running your indie publishing or traditional writing career, and allows you to sleep at night knowing you have not forgotten the work you need or want to accomplish.

1.2 Gathering your to-do list tools

Before starting to work on your list, you need to assemble the tools that will help you accomplish your tasks. You won't need many. I recommend you try the suggested tools listed and then later, once you have some experience with the process, begin to investigate alternatives as you look for ways to continue to improve your approach.

Here is a list of tools to use as you develop your to-do list process. Start with these and then expand the list, or revise it as you see fit. You will need:

1) An application for storing your to-do list – I recommend Todoist. There is a free version and a premium version that is very reasonably priced. The latest pricing is found at: www.todoist.com.

2) An email program – use whichever email program you currently use

3) A calendar application – Use your current program

4) A document management system for storing information – I recommend Evernote. **www.evernote.com**

5) I am an Evernote Certified Consultant. If you need help with Evernote, email me at **TPrice@TonyaPrice.com**.

6) A paper reminder system – Despite all the cool apps available, sometimes it is helpful to dash off a note on paper.

7) Post-it Notes – They will be part of your daily reminder process.

8) A whiteboard – we will discuss how to use it, but you do not need one.

If you think some of these items overlap, you are right! We will soon see how they form a system to keep you on top of your workload. First, let's review how these tools can help us get things done.

1.3 Computer/mobile applications we'll use

While you can make a list on paper of all your to-do list items, you always risk losing the paper copy or leaving it on your desk while traveling. Many writers find it easier to use applications to store, track and archive items they need to complete. Others use a combination of desktop and mobile apps with a paper backup. Some people collect their list in their email application, although it is not easy to organize your deadlines using email, and many email programs lack any reminder notice capability.

Writers respond differently to organizational strategies so we will review a variety of methods. Your job is to become familiar with what is available and use this book to find out which combination of tools and tactics work best for you. An approach will be described that will get you started that over time, you refine to create an approach that works best for you.

Many items that need to be tracked are related to the writing and production of a book (for example, the various steps in a marketing plan). In such cases, the tasks make up a single project. They are best tracked as a whole since each task impacts the remaining things to be done. Some applications allow you to create a project and keep all the tasks together; permitting you to track deadlines for both the individual items and the overall project delivery date.

One sign that your tasks are too broadly defined is when you have trouble starting on them. Writers find complicated items hard to begin; however, if you break the task into smaller to-do items, it will become less intimidating, and you will find it easier to start.

Once you have a manageable list of everything you want to accomplish, group tasks into broad categories such as:

- Write the book
- Publish the book
- Market the book

You can then break each category into smaller parts. For example, "Write the book" divides into:

- Research
- Outline
- Write
- Edit

There may be additional steps depending on whether you are submitting your work to an agent or are self-publishing the work. As my good friend, author Carlos Valcarcel points out organizing your work into groups helps you identify if you have left out any steps in your book project. If you struggle with organizing the writing of your books you might want to read *Meeting the Writer's Deadline*,[4] which reviews how to manage book projects.

You want to assign a deadline and schedule completion dates based on when the first task begins, and the last, related item ends. Related tasks often comprise a project. Examples of a project containing a number of steps to be finished by a deadline include: creating a marketing calendar, starting an indie publishing business or writing a book.

Each task is a project, composed of a series of steps, where some requirements are dependent on completing other actions. Therefore you want an app that can let you group these to-dos and follow them as single components of the overall project.

1.4 Applications for managing to-do lists

Several programs meet the requirements listed above. We will use Todoist.

Installation options: Todoist is cloud-based and offers mobile versions for both iPhone and Android that can sync with the desktop version. You can choose between a free version and a pro version.

Authors often avoid web-based programs out of privacy concerns and a desire to prevent hacking issues.

Premium vs. Free version: If you want to avoid a cloud-based application, the premium version of Todoist allows you to work offline and to email tasks to Todoist. This is a useful feature for tasks such as: renew your association membership fee or cancel your one-year auto-renew subscription for an application you no longer want.

Integration with other tools: many programs sync with Todoist, which, if you don't mind using web-based applications, can make Todoist a powerful tool; but Todoist by itself has all the requirements that we need for efficient task collection and can be used off-line.

Choices: An up-to-date list of additional programs is on the Business Books For Writers Tools web page.

1.5 Email Program – Use your favorite

Email is one way you:

1) Receive tasks you need to complete
2) Delegate items you can offload to your production team
3) Delete work from your Inbox that you do NOT need to do

Almost any email program will work. Many people use Microsoft Outlook because they learned it at work. Apple Mail is another popular option, as is Google Mail.

Make sure your email program can filter messages and create folders. All the programs mentioned above have this feature.

1.6 Calendar program

You will need a good calendar program for tracking your appointments and events.

The calendar program that you use doesn't matter. iCal, Fantastical2, Outlook, and Google calendar are popular options. You want to be able to set reminders and to import emails into the program.

For those who don't mind web-based applications and want to have their list handy at all times, the ability to sync between your smartphone, desktop, laptop, tablet, or smart watch can be a nice wish-list feature.

1.7 Paper tools

You might think that with all the electronic tools we have, a paper system is redundant. However, using paper is our fail-safe solution. The physical exercise of writing down your to-do list for the next day rather than typing the information decreases the chance of you forgetting a task you need to complete. I know it is hard to believe (I didn't believe it either until I started trying it!) This approach made such a difference for me I encourage you to try it too if you find you type things into files but still occasionally forget about tasks you need to accomplish.

Remember: don't be afraid to experiment

If you see something you don't think will work for you, try these recommendations and then experiment with tweaking them to fit your needs.

1.8 Pad of paper on your desk beside your computer

You are in the middle of writing a chapter and bam; you get a brilliant idea for marketing the book. You could open a new word doc, type in the info, save the file and go back to work. Or, you can send yourself a quick email with the idea. Many writers find it less disruptive to have a pad of paper on their desk where they can jot a quick note.

I have found it much less disruptive and less likely to divert me from the writing at hand to make a quick reminder on the notepad. When I've completed my work, I go back and email myself the idea.

1.9 Post-it notes

Many writers find they write the actions they intend to complete on paper and input them in apps that can be viewed on their desktop and mobile devices and still, forget to complete the tasks (both writing and non-writing) that needed to be done that day.

I solved this problem with Post-It Notes. I like the arrow-shaped notes to stick on the side of my computer screen as a constant reminder during the day of what I want to accomplish, but any sticky note will work. Write one to-do per note, and when completed you get the satisfaction of throwing away the paper knowing you've completed the task (never underestimate the power of dopamine spikes).

1.10 Mini-notebooks

Everyone uses a mobile device these days, but there are times when you may find it awkward to use a cell phone. For this reason, I recommend you also purchase a mini-notebook and carry it with you at all times as recommended by Stephen Covey in his book, *The 7 Habits of Highly Effective People.*[5]

I am someone who does everything on a computer or cell phone, and I can't believe how much I use my mini-notebook. There are times writing things down in a mini-notebooks makes conversations quicker than electronic capturing methods, and there are times when those electronic devices have no charge. Either way, you can still write down your new task or new idea.

You do not need an expensive notebook. You can get affordable ones at the Dollar Tree stores.

Chapter 1 Points to remember

1) Form the habit of capturing, tracking, maintaining, and completing your to-do list.

2) Recognize that you will get behind on your to-do list at some point, but commit to returning to your process and refuse to give up tracking your to-dos.

3) Before developing your list process have a to-do list application similar to Todoist; an email program; a calendar program and/or your preferred paper tool for quick notes/reminders

Next Step: Capturing tasks for your master list

In Chapter 2, you will prepare for gathering all your action items into one master list.

PART 2: PREPARING FOR SUCCESS

Chapter 2: Capturing Your Tasks

Many writers scribble what they want to accomplish on scraps of paper, embed goals in emails stored in folders, or enter the work they need to complete into one or more to-do apps during their attempts to organize their work. They lose the paper, can never find the emails and will go weeks without opening their organization app.

The first step in gaining control of your tasks is to gather everything you need to do in one list, so you always know where to go to find the work to be done.

You cannot possibly remember everything you need to do without a system for tracking everything you need to accomplish. If you form the habit of always following your process, you will complete all your goals on time.

2.1 Create a single list of everything you need to complete

If you are not currently using a to-do list management app or program, sign up for Todoist.

Tip: Have you tried an application to handle your task list but abandoned it?

There are a lot of programs that track to-do items. If you have used a program only to abandon it, I recommend you try Todoist and compare both applications before deciding which to use. Todoist is simple to use and integrates with other programs. You can set reminders by date/time and get your reminder through email, notifications or with a push reminder to your phone. (Note: I get no commission from recommending Todoist, I just think it is a good application.)

Even if you prefer a paper-based or whiteboard-based approach to tracking everything you need to track, you will want to read through the basics of managing your list on the following pages to learn new techniques you can implement in your process.

Before you read any further, take the time to collect all the work action items you need to finish and put them into Todoist. We will sort through them later. For now, we want to avoid having any of your tasks drop through the cracks and be forgotten.

2.2 List where you currently store or receive action items

If you don't currently keep your tasks in one location, make a checklist of every place you might find a project you need to tackle. Places to check include:

- Email
- Paper lists
- Notepads on your desk
- A mini notebook that you carry with you
- Scraps of paper (I have a friend who uses the back of envelopes to jot down what she needs to get done – a habit that can lead to your list being accidentally thrown out with the trash, as her husband has done more than once).
- Calendar invites
- Meeting notes
- Whiteboards
- Information you have been keeping in your head
- Add any other places you might have written down list items

2.3 Optional: Create a labeling system

You can use labels to quickly find action items that are similar. You won't need labels if your to-do list is small, but if you have a lengthy list, then labels can save you a lot of time otherwise spent looking for that action item you know you need to complete, but can't find.

Some people are used to labeling and love it. The description of labeling is covered before the lesson on capturing your tasks to provide the information necessary for those people who would like to label their action items as they create their master list.

You can always create your master list and then go back and create labels for your tasks.

2.4 Labeling your action items

If you haven't used a labeling system, you may find that trying to start using labels a bit intimidating while you are trying to set up a new process for handling your action list. Read this section and decide if you want to incorporate these ideas now, or if you want to hold off.

How do you know if you would benefit from using a labeling system with your to-do items? The easy answer is when you find yourself spending so much time looking for an activity that you want to work on that you are using precious minutes you could be devoting to getting the work done; you should consider setting up a labeling system.

Label or Tags: what are they and how do you use them?

You need to be able to find the work you need to complete. Labels (called "tags" in some programs like Word) make your tasks easier to find since you can search for the word that describes the category. You will receive the list of items assigned to the tag.

How labels work in Todoist

Note: Labels are not included in the free version of Todoist.

When you open Todoist, you see your Inbox – today and Next 7 days listed vertically on the left side of your screen.

Underneath this list, you see Projects. To the right of Projects, you see greyed out the word, "Labels" and then "Filters." If you wish to use labels and filters you will need to purchase the premium version.

How to create a Label for your task (premium version of Todoist)

Step 1: Click on the grey Labels heading.

Step 2: Click on the yellow "+ Add Label."

Step 3: Create a label titled, "Urgent."

Common labels to start with might be:

- Urgent
- This month
- Next month
- Waiting for action
- Archive
- Read and delete

Some people like to use more specific labels like an Event name or Family; Business; or Conventions.

You can create whatever naming structure you want, but it is best to give some thought to how you will use your labels and stick to that format. That is why I recommend that you start out simple and add more later.

For now, use the labels above if you are new to using labels.

If all your labels come out the same color, just click on the label icon next to your label text. You will get a chart of 13 colors to choose from. Using different colors can make it easy to see at a glance the type item you are looking at.

The benefit of labels

Create two more tasks and attach the label "Urgent" to those items.

Now, click on Labels in the left sidebar.

Every task with the label Urgent appears.

Create a task in Todoist by going to the very top of the Todoist window. You will see a plus sign (+) which when you click on it creates a new task.

After you create your new task, you will see it appear at the bottom of your task list. Click on the task name. Now you see an orange Save button, Cancel and to the right five icons: calendar; Label; a clock; a flag and three dots.

Click on the Label icon. The list of labels you have created comes up.

Downloads

You can download a list of common tags writers use from the Business Books for Writers website at:

www.BusinessBooksForWriters.com/To-Do_Downloads

The download file will contain:

- A flowchart of the To-Do List Process described in the book
- A list of common labels or tags to use when you start out using tags
- Screen shots of how to create labels in Todoist

More information on using labels with Todoist

Todoist offers an extensive support area with videos, instructions and lots of information to help you make the most of their tool. If you would like to learn more about how Todoist labels can increase your productivity visit

https://blog.todoist.com/user-stories/9-ways-to-use-todoist-labels-filters/

For more information on creating TodoIst labels visit

https://support.todoist.com/hc/en-us/articles/205195042-Labels

Chapter 2 Points to remember

1) Choose a place to keep your master to-do list.

2) Make a list of every place you might have stored an action item.

3) Todoist labels can help you manage a long to-do list.

Next Step: Compile your list

In Chapter 3 we will create your master list by gathering all the action items you have stored in the places listed in Chapter 2.

Chapter 3: Compiling Your Master List

In Chapter 2, you listed everywhere you might find an action item that you have not worked on yet. We need to get all those tasks in one master list, so you know exactly what you need to do.

Going forward, you will keep everything that needs to be done on this list. One advantage of this approach is that you always know where to go to find what you need to do. If a life event interferes with your ability to work on completing your tasks update, you can find all your action items in your master list rather than hunting through multiple places for a to-do item.

I have had this happen to me several times either as a result of an illness or having to care for a family member. Even happy occasions like a wedding can throw you off your task management process for a while. If this happens don't think that the process doesn't work, recognize that life sometimes forces us off track once in a while and we can we have to pick ourselves up and get back to work.

3.1 Look for tasks in your email accounts

If you have an agent and an editor you probably get the bulk of assigned tasks in email. Many self-publishers use email as a way of recording something you should do or want to do. Your production team may exchange updates through email.

You need to capture these items in your master action list.

Go through each of your email accounts and find work that you need to do.

Create an "Add Task" in Todoist for any action items you find in your email accounts and add the task. Remember you can send action items that need attention to Todoist if you have the premium version. (I find this to be a valuable time-saving feature). Otherwise, you can copy and paste the email text into a new Todoist task.

If you have more than one email account, repeat this process for any account where you receive tasks to complete.

Congratulations! You now have a master list of everything you need to do that was previously buried in your various mail accounts. The system we are going to set up will capture your tasks as they arise. You will not need to go through this process and creating a master task list again unless a major life event causes you to get behind.

3.2 Collect your calendar appointments and events

Let's take a look at your calendar.

You need to give everything you want to complete a start date and a deadline.

Do you have notes on your calendar appointments that involve tasks you must complete for meetings? If so, add those to your master task list in Todoist.

Next, check your meeting notes from any ongoing meetings you have such as weekly co-author meetings, or writing buddy meetings. Are you an officer of an association chapter, such as Sisters in Crime or Romance Writers of America?

Add any tasks you need to complete to the list.

Enter events such as conferences you must attend on your calendar, as these are action items that must be completed too.

Also, add tasks relating to any marketing materials you might want to have on hand for the next conference you are attending, such as bookmark creation and production, ad buys, giveaways, ordering extra copies of your book to give away, or contacting booksellers to carry your book. Maybe you want to autograph books before the conference. Add ordering the books to your list and then add autograph the books as a separate action item.

TIP: Group related to-do items into a project

When you are preparing to attend a conference, put all of the related marketing tasks for the conference into a project. By lumping them together, you may see relationships and possibilities for grouping items you hadn't thought of before.

3.3 Review your whiteboards

A lot of writers (including me) love whiteboards. If you have to-do items on your whiteboard, add them to your master list.

3.4 Check your paper lists

I listed various types of paper tools where you might jot down to-do list tasks in the previous chapter. Go through your mini-notebook, the pad of paper on your desk, any notebooks or journals you used to catch tasks you must complete.

Add these to your master to-do list.

3.5 Add the information you have been keeping in your head

Finally, take some time to think about tasks you need to complete, but haven't because you keep forgetting to start the work required. You probably won't remember all the to-do list items you have stored in your head, but write down those you can remember right now. You can add the others to the list later, as you remember them.

David Allen in his book, "Getting Things Done: The Art of Stress-Free Productivity"[6] has a long list of what he calls, "incompletion triggers" to be used when trying to empty your head of all the action items you might not have written down. If you know you have tasks in your head that you can't remember, you might want to check out his list.

Congratulations! Now you have a comprehensive master to-do list! You will not forget any of the important tasks you need to undertake as long as you refer to this list and keep it updated.

Chapter 3 Points to remember

1) You gain control over your tasks by recording them in one place. You lose track of items when you don't maintain a master list.

2) Maintain your master list in a Todoist or a similar program.

3) When you are organizing your list for the first time, or after having let it lapse for a while, follow the process we used in this chapter to create or update a master list of all your action items.

Next Step: How to use tags/labels

In Chapter 4, we will learn about how to use tags and how they can help you find action items quickly. Then we will clean up your master action item list.

PART 3: DEVELOPING A SYSTEM THAT WORKS FOR YOU

Chapter 4: Organizing Your Master List

When moving your action items into your master list consider adding one of the tags that you created earlier to the item to help you determine the order you want to complete your tasks.

Now that you have your master to-do list in one place, you need to decide what you will do with each of the items on your list and assign each task a deadline.

David Allen introduced the idea of spending no more than two minutes evaluating work you must do and then taking action by Completing, Deleting, Deferring or Delegating each task. Let's take a look at how to use this idea to conquer your email.

4.1 Work on tasks that you can complete in two minutes or less

Review each task in your master list. Complete any item you can finish in two minutes or less. For example, if you have a note that says, "Let your cover designer know your book's ISBN," send a quick email with the ISBN and move to the next email.

When you encounter an item that requires more than two minutes to complete, determine if this is a task that still needs to be completed or if it can be deleted.

4.2 Delete

Delete any item that you completed or any tasks with a missed deadline that will not be done in the future.

4.3 Delegate

If the task still needs to be done determine if it can be delegated to someone else. All writers, whether traditionally published or self-published, must have a website, conduct online marketing and social media marketing. However, this work can be outsourced.

Evaluate whether it is cost effective for you to hire someone to do a task for you. (One great resource for this type of work is a service like **Fiverr.com** where you can choose from a variety of professionals to do marketing, web design or social media work for you at affordable prices.)

4.4 Defer work until later

If you cannot delegate a task through outsourcing, ask yourself if you can defer the work until a later date?

By applying this evaluation process to each task, you will be left with a master list of work that you need to tackle.

4.5 Assign a deadline to every task

Go through your master list and assign a deadline to any item that does not already have a due date.

Some list items will not have a due date. Assign an end date anyway. Any work that lacks an assigned completion period lingers undone because something will always arise that carries a higher priority. A deadline gives tasks a priority that, over time, will rise as you either face pressure to complete work you owe other people, such as write a guest blog, or realize that by not doing these tasks you are negatively impacting your business and reputation.

An example of the latter would be your decision to create a Pinterest account for raising your brand's awareness. Think how easy it would be to put this off indefinitely, yet it could have big benefits in growing awareness among readers that would like and buy your books — if they knew they existed.

An app like Todoist allows you to identify when an action item is due. You can set pop-up reminders, or you can have the program send you an email reminder.

> ## TIP: Automatically have your list deadlines go to your calendar
>
> If you find that you never remember to open Todoist, you can choose to have Todoist automatically load all your project due dates in your calendar. Learn how at https://support.todoist.com/hc/en-us/articles/208789889. Last viewed January 31, 2018.

Chapter 4 Points to remember

1) Follow David Allen's rule of examining every email that requires an action on your part and either do it, delegate it, defer it or delete it.

2) Always assign a deadline to every task you need to finish.

3) Sync Todoist with your calendar will get notifications or email reminders of your project deadlines.

Next Step: Your process for controlling tasks

In Chapter 5 you will learn a process for completing your clean to-do master list and for handling new tasks.

Chapter 5: Establishing Your To-do List

You created a master list with every action item you need to complete. The next step is to create a process for dealing with your deferred work and new action items to ensure you complete everything on time.

5.1 The process

The key to getting your action list under control is to follow a routine for handling the work you need to complete each day. In the beginning, use the process discussed in this chapter for a few weeks. If you struggle with the recommended schedule due to the demands of your day job or family commitments, change your approach. Find a schedule that works better for you — but once you discover an approach that works, continue your process daily.

Above all, remember the KISS principle – Keep it Simple, Stupid! The more complicated your plan, the more likely you are to stop using it.

In order to be successful as a writing entrepreneur you need to complete all the work that supports writing books, producing your books or short stories or articles (whether through a traditional publisher or by self-publishing your work), marketing your work so people know your book exists, and completing the administrative tasks required of any business.

In order to handle these many tasks you need to:

- Capture every task you need to complete
- Identify a deadline for every action item
- Decide which actions you are going to work on each day
- Review your list to make sure you have the order correct for completing the work
- Review what you have accomplished, what you want to accomplish, future projects and what you will work on today

5.2 Establish a schedule

One key to completing all the work you need to finish is to set up the following:

1) **Start of day review time** to remind yourself what you are going to work on during the day
2) **Scheduled time on your calendar** for actually doing the work
3) **End of day review time** to verify you didn't forget anything

4) **Next day planning time** to determine the order you will do your work what you need to complete to meet your deadlines

TIP: Set up your schedule now

If you are able, take a break and using your calendar, create blocks of time for your schedule right now.

A typical schedule might be:

8:00 am – 8:15 am: Start of day review time

8:15 – 8:30 am: review email (Chapter 9 discusses how to manage your emails and will have more on how to use this time.)

11:00 am-noon: work on action item 1

12:30 – 1:00 pm: review new emails for the day. If any require an urgent task, schedule the work for time reserved for action item 2. Push action item 2 to action item 3's slot and reschedule action item 3 for the next day.

1:00 – 2:00 pm: work on action item 2

3:00 – 4:00 pm: work on action item 3

4:30 – 5:00 pm: review your email list

8:30 – 9:00 pm: Identify three action items for tomorrow, schedule when you will work on them based on the time needed to complete them, enter them into Todoist and create three sticky notes for your monitor and put them on your monitor now or in the morning.

If you are working at a day job in a hectic environment such a precise schedule might be impossible to maintain. Be creative and come up with a schedule that is possible to follow. For example, check your email while on the train going to work, at noon during your lunch and on the train commuting home. Even if you miss the lunch email check, you can still catch up at the end of the day.

Vary the times, not the steps

Even if you work at home and are operating as a self-publisher completely independent of anyone else, as soon as you start to become successful, you will start finding that other people will impact your daily schedule.

An editor decides to retire, and you get a notice he needs your completed manuscript a week earlier than he said. You get invited to speak at Malice Domestic, and it is the week you were going to deliver that romance writers webinar.

No one becomes successful by themselves. (That is a topic for another book!) Other people will throw off your daily schedule. What do you do when this happens?

Don't panic. Reschedule your tasks for the day. Take five minutes and decide how to rearrange them.

If you are not yet earning a full-time living as a writing entrepreneur, you will have less flexibility in your schedule. The irony is that once you do become successful as a writer you will find you have less flexibility in your schedule as editors, book tours, webinar opportunities, etc. intrude on your schedule. If you find you have to work late to finish that team project that is due in a week, then, when you get home complete that task you were going to do at lunchtime.

If this happens repeatedly, alter your schedule to find one that works for you.

5.3 The rule of three

No matter the length of your list you want to make your daily list manageable. If you have twenty things due tomorrow, then before you start working on your process you need to negotiate new deadlines for your to-do items.

The "rule of 3" is from J. D. Meier's book, *Getting Results the Agile Way*.[7] The first writer who recommended this method of handling to-do items to me was the romantic-suspense author, M.L. Buchman. **www.mlbuchman.com**

The approach is simple, but it keeps your to-do list from being overwhelming.

When using the rule of 3, break down your to-do list into the following steps:

1) Identify three things you want to accomplish tomorrow.

2) Identify three goals you want to accomplish this week.

3) Write down three goals you want to accomplish this month.

Grow your business by setting yearly goals

I am an advocate for setting yearly goals as will to grow your business. As writers, we can work twenty-four hours a day and still not accomplish everything we would like to get done. Since we are creative people, we can always think of additional work we could take on that would help us grow our business, or another book that we would like to write or another media we would like to explore.

Be aware that you can accomplish a great many tasks that do nothing to help your business grow. Yearly goals remind you of your chosen strategy for making the money that will allow you to pursue your business without losing money. When you are working on your to-do list, there will be action items you must accomplish, but try to make sure that at least one action item every day will help you achieve your business goals. Examples of business goals might be:

- Write three books this year
- Publish one audio book version for each ebook and print book
- Reduce your book production cost by ten percent

Yearly goals helps you create a reasonable schedule for the year, but it also forces you to be more focused on what you want to accomplish. Your aspirations for the year should be ambitious objectives that will drive your strategy. They need to be SMART goals. That means that they should be:

- **S**pecific: well-defined goal
- **M**easurable: you can measure your progress
- **A**ttainable: Is it possible to reach your goal?
- **R**elevant: Does it make sense to pursue the goal and fit with your strategy?
- **T**imely: the goals are achievable within a specified timeframe

You can read more about SMART goals and goal setting strategies in *Meeting the Writer's Deadline.*[8]

5.4 Keep your to-do list in front of you

Even after you have sorted your master list, it may be quite long. A long list can feel overwhelming. While many writers track their tasks electronically, some writers find if they store a list of what they need to accomplish in an electronic file, they forget to look at the list and they lose track of work that needs to be done.

We will discuss how a review process can help you maintain your list; but often, the best way to remember to work on your to-dos is to physically write down your to-dos for the day and keep them in front of you.

You want to see the list during the day so that even if you are interrupted by a phone call or an urgent email when you sit back down at your desk, you will get back on track and finish everything before the end of the day.

Authors may use a whiteboard to keep their to-do items visible. Others write on a pad of paper that sits on the desk beside a computer monitor or keyboard. Some writers use a Day Runner or similar notebook system to plot out their schedule, goals, and to-dos on paper before committing them to electronic programs.

You want to keep your to-do list where you can see it. For this reason, I write down the three things that I want to accomplish the next day on the sticky arrows that I put on my monitor; and the three things for the week, month, and year on a whiteboard that I can see from my desk.

I put the three sticky notes on the side of my large desktop monitor. When I finish an item, I pull it off the computer display, crumple it up and throw it away, then mark my electronic to-do as "Done!"

TIP: Use sticky memo notes or arrows to remember your daily to-do list items.

Take a look at the Bags for Less 2000 Sticky Note/Flag Organizer Black for a nice set of color-coordinated sticky notes and arrows.

Assign a time period on your calendar for working on each of your three task items. Calendar entries help you to remember what you need to get done.

Creating an entry for to-do tasks on your calendar requires knowing how much time approximately you will need to complete your to-do list item. Predicting how long you will need is not always possible, especially if you are tackling a task you have never tried before. In such a case, estimate the time you think it will take to complete a task. Over time when you have to perform a similar action, your estimate will be more accurate as you learn from experience.

5.5 Your Daily Routine

Start your writing workday with your morning start of the day review time you identified earlier. Read through your to-do list for the day to keep it fresh in your mind. Looking over your list first thing will remind you of the work you intended to complete.

Check your email

Most people check their email too often. At one point in history, postal mail delivery came once a month. Then people received their mail once a week. Today some people check their email every five minutes. Choose three times during the day when you will manage your email. Schedule your first review in the morning after looking over your day's to-do list.

As you review each message apply David Allen's organizational formula we discussed earlier to your emails: Do it (if under 2 minutes to complete), Delete, Delegate, or Defer.

1) Delete emails requiring no action that you don't want to keep.

2) Forward delegated emails to Todoist after you send your comments to someone on your team. (To forward an email find the gray icon just to the right of your note title. The cursor turns black when crossing over the icon. Click and add any instructions to the action. In the comment section indicate the name of the person assigned the task, the day and time you delegated the action, and the agreed-upon due date.) Always assign a deadline to every item you need to complete.

3) Add deferred emails containing tasks to pursue as a new To-do item in Todoist.

Check your voicemail

Apply the same do, delete, defer or delegate process to voicemail.

Writers who have day jobs

Writers who are working full-time regular jobs might start writing at 5:30 am or 7:00 pm, around their work schedules. Whenever you start your writing day, take five minutes to look over your to-do list first, so you spend your precious writing time working on the tasks you most need to do for your writing success.

Often we have the impression that the email that we just received is what we need to do immediately, but that might not be true. Review your list each night and determine the three more important tasks you want to complete the next day. Often the item you just added to the list — but which isn't due for a week — is less critical than the to-do list item that has been slowly working its way to the top of your list for the past four days.

TIP: For those who write before they do anything else for the day

Do you prefer to write first thing in the morning? If so, then review your to-do list right after you finish writing.

Break time check-in

Writing breaks provide an opportunity to review your remaining to-do list for the day. If you use Pomodoro, your Pomodoro breaks are a good time for this. (If you are not familiar with the Pomodoro technique, check out this website: Productivity 101: A Primer to the Pomodoro Technique, **bit.ly/2qbr0Py**.

Good apps to use with the Pomodoro method are Focus Time or Be Focused Pro on the Mac **https://xwavesoft.com/be-focused-pro-for-iphone-ipad-**

mac-os-x.html or FocusBooster for Windows. **www.focusboosterapp.com**.

Check your email three times a day

Emails can take a lot of unplanned time during the workday. Therefore, continue to handle emails as you did when you established your initial to-do list.

1) Check your email no more than three times during your day: first thing in the morning, at lunch, and at the end of your writing workday. Schedule this time on your calendar program.

2) When you are reviewing your email, turn off the Wi-Fi connection. You will get more done if you only work on email that you have not received. Getting emails while working on emails leads to working on multiple email messages at the same time. Chapter 9 describes an approach for keeping your email manageable. Do a quick scan of the messages and look for Important and Urgent tasks. If you find one, reassess whether to elevate the new action item a higher priority than the remaining tasks on your list for the day.

3) Subject each email to the 2 minutes to complete, otherwise delete, defer, or delegate your messages using the system described at the beginning of this chapter. Flag any emails you defer so you can capture them as new activities to add to Todoist.

Voice Mail

Let calls go to voicemail during your writing time. After you have gone through your email (or before based on how you like to work), listen to your voicemail. Apply the same approach to sorting voicemail that you used with email: complete-in-2-minutes, delete, defer, or delegate.

End of day review time

When you have finished your writing day, complete any to-dos that are not complete. There will be days when you don't complete all three to-dos on your list. That is why many writers work on the most important task first. Unfinished to-dos will migrate to the top of your list.

Before you quit for the day, create your to-do list for the next day. Start your list of three to-do items with any current to-do items you deferred from the day before. Go to your Day Runner or calendar program and estimate how much time you require to complete each task, and then reserve slots in your schedule for the work.

Whatever time you pick, do this review every day at the same time (or as close to the same time as is realistically possible), so this exercise becomes a habit. If you follow this approach, you will start each day working immediately on what you need to get done rather than wasting time thinking about what you need to do.

5.6 Tasks that wake you up at night

Many writers find that as soon as they go to bed, they remember all the tasks they needed to complete. The Soviet psychologist, Bluma Wulfovna Zeigarnik, discovered in 1927 that our brains are wired to forget completed tasks but to remember uncompleted tasks.

When you start to go to sleep, the brain goes through everything you don't need to remember from the day and sorts out what you do need to remember. If you write down what you need to remember before you go to bed, then your brain doesn't need to remember your to-do list that is a completed task.

Try it! I have found that this technique works for me. I can fall asleep knowing that when I wake all the work I need to do is captured in my to-do master list. Rather than worrying about what I need to do, I just work on doing the items on my list!

You can read more about this phenomenon at Psychologist World, "The Zeigarnik Effect Explained."[9]

TIP: When you wake up during the night thinking of task you need to complete:

As soon as you lay down to go to sleep, you inevitably remember that email you keep forgetting to write, or that great blog you read that sparked a marketing idea you want to integrate into your business plan. Keep paper beside your bed. If you get ideas after you have gone to bed, you can write them down and add them to your list in the morning.

There are three ways to record what you want to accomplish the next day: use a voicemail app to record your ideas, have a pad of paper on the nightstand that you use to write the ideas down or send yourself a quick email with just the action item in the subject.

To-do items often come in the middle of the night. If you read through your to-do list before you go to bed, your brain is less likely to wake you up with an item you have forgotten.

5.7 Your review schedule

Weekly Review

Set up time at the end of every work week to review your to-do list for the upcoming week. A good time for this review is during the last work hour on Friday or Sunday evening. Look over your email, voicemail, calendar, and the small notepad you carry with you for those hallway conversations. Capture any action items you may have missed during the week and recheck their due dates. Verify that your Todoist list includes every action you need to complete during the upcoming week.

Monthly Review

As we mentioned earlier, tasks that do not have a deadline generally get forgotten or are delayed. To catch any tasks that may have fallen into this situation, do a monthly review of your task list.

The last working day of the month is a good time to schedule this review. Unless you assign these to-do items a due date these tasks can easily linger for days, weeks, or months before they get completed. If you need to, you can defer them to the following month, but often these chores will help grow your business. You hurt your business if they remain undone. Rather than defer them repeatedly, assign a due date and make these actions a priority.

Six-month review

Some writers also like to conduct a biennial review of their to-do list as well as the monthly and yearly review. This six-month check-in will help you evaluate the chances of you accomplishing your goals. Add the time on your calendar to go over your six-month goals, too.

Yearly review

Be sure to review your long-term goals at least once a year. Pick a meaningful day. I do my review on New Year's Day. Many writers like to look back on what they have accomplished when they are on a yearly vacation, the anniversary of their company founding or during their December holiday break. In your writer's business plan, you have scheduled a yearly review to go over your goals for the year and entered this date into your calendar. This review is the perfect time to come up with a yearly list of tasks to be completed the coming year such as:

- Create next year's marketing schedule
- Create next year's advertising schedule
- Create next year's budget for marketing, education, research, conferences, book production, etc.
- Identify yearly tasks to perform. My second-year goals were: hit 1000 email subscribers, publish five new books and create ways to benefit three influencers.

5.8 Should you prioritize your to-do list?

Determining to-do list priorities can be difficult when you first start going through your tasks. The rule of 3 will help you stay focused on tackling a manageable amount of to-do items in one day (people fail when they try to catch up all at once).
Let's look at three ways to prioritize your list:

1) Start with your most important task as discussed in chapter one. You will sometimes see this term in articles this capitalized and referred to as MIT.

2) Prioritize tasks as they come up (this can be very hard to do if you have a very long catch-up to-do list to tackle)

3) Use the Eisenhower Quadrant Method

Option 1: MIT – Most Important Task approach

Using the Most Important Task approach, identify one thing you must get done each day. That is the thing you will do before you quit working that day.

Some days, one thing is all you can accomplish. There will be times when you don't finish your MIT in a day, but at least you have identified the most important task and made some progress towards meeting your goal. If your MIT requires several days or weeks, verify that you are working on one action item and not a series of action items that comprise a project. List each task in a project separately, even though you track them as part of your project. You are more likely to complete the project on time if you concentrate on one action item at a time.

After you identify your MIT, then pick the next two most critical tasks to work on after you get your MIT done.

Some writers prefer to eat their dessert first; some prefer to eat it last. Whether you are the kind of person who likes to get the hardest task out of the way or if you prefer to tackle the easy tasks first, you want to make sure you get that MIT done by its deadline.

REMEMBER: Your MIT is the most critical task you need to get done

Your MIT is not the longest, most involved, or most complicated task on your list, but the one that you must complete by its deadline.

You can combine the MIT and priority approaches. Identify your most important task, then rank remaining actions for the week according to importance or due date. Select two additional to-do items for the day in case you complete the list. Some authors like to include at least one non-critical, but fun, item on their daily to-do list. This approach lessens the stress of the workday if your schedule has time for this strategy.

Consider scheduling your most important tasks early in the week. If you get behind, the less important items can be pushed to the following week. You can only do this with action items that do not have a critical deadline the week they are scheduled.

Option 2: Tackle to-dos as they arise

This approach works best when you have a long list, and everything is labeled MIT. When everything is critical, and the priorities for each task are the same, this approach says, take the stress out of worrying about which is the most important task — instead, just set a deadline for each task, and complete the tasks before their deadline.

If you use this approach, you still want to limit yourself to three tasks a day.

Can you do more than three tasks a day? Absolutely, but only schedule three tasks. You want to end the day feeling successful. If you complete your three items and find yourself with time to do more, then go to your weekly or monthly list and select an additional task to add to your day's workload.

5.9 The Eisenhower Quadrant

The Eisenhower quadrant is a visual tool for determining the priority of work you need to tackle for the day. The basic idea is to use a diagram to show the relative importance of each task and its urgency. In reality, it is a simple approach, and as was said earlier, simple is best when it comes task lists.

How to use the quadrant

To create an Eisenhower quadrant or matrix, draw a square and then divide it into four squares. Label the top left quadrant "Important but Not Urgent." Title the top right quadrant "Important and Urgent." Designate the bottom left quadrant "Not Important and Not Urgent," and the bottom right quadrant, "Urgent but Not Important."

Sort your week's to-do items into the quadrants.

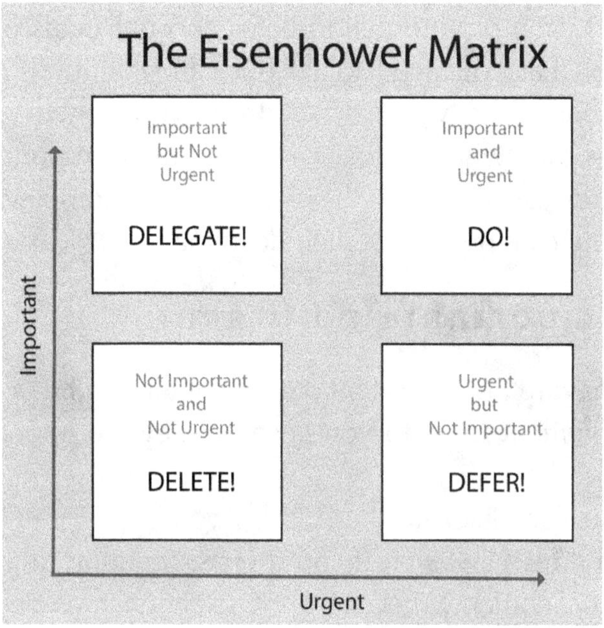
The Eisenhower Matrix
Important
but Not
Urgent
DELEGATE!
Important
and
Urgent
DO!
Not Important
and
Not Urgent
DELETE!
Urgent
but
Not Important
DEFER!
Important
Urgent

Example of an Eisenhower Quadrant
(image created by Tonya D. Price)

Important & Urgent - your MITs go here

Once you complete the "do-in-under-2-minutes, delete, delegate, or defer" process, you should have only MIT items left for this quadrant.

Important & Not Urgent

There will always be some tasks, which are important, but are not urgent. These are often tasks without deadlines. You need to give these to-dos deadlines and schedule them, or they will linger unfinished. Review the deadlines you have assigned each of your action items and put items into this quadrant that you need to do but can schedule for later. Remember, since you have a deadline attached to these activities they will eventually move into the Important and Urgent category. If you have a chance, complete them before they are up against their deadline.

Not Important and Urgent

Tasks that are not important but urgent tend to be tasks that have been delegated to you because they are important to someone else.

If you can delegate these tasks, you will certainly save yourself time. However, if you do pass them on to a virtual assistant, another writer, or an association member, track them. Often these requests come without deadlines. Assigning a due date to these actions. By ensuring that these requests are finished you will be helping your reputation and earning yourself a grateful contact, who may someday offer to assist you with your Important and Urgent to-do items. (Remember, to them this future task will be a Not Important and Urgent task!)

Not Important and Not Urgent

If an action is not important and not urgent, you should delete it from your master list. Actually, it should only appear if it was once in one of the other categories and then it's priority or importance changed. Reviewing the master list periodically will help you spot those tasks that are no longer needed and can be dropped from the list.

TIP: There are apps, which simplify using the Eisenhower Quadrant

- Focus Matrix: Mac, iPhone, iPad
- TaskCracker: Included in Microsoft Outlook
- PriorityMatrix by Appfluence: Windows, MAC, iPhone, and Android
- Eisenhower: Web-based app

Dependent to-dos

Tasks made up of several smaller tasks are projects. "Write a novel" is not a to-do list item but a book project. The idea of writing a book can be an intimidating exercise to anyone who knows all that goes into the process. The way to make the project less intimidating is to break large tasks into individual to-do items.

1) Generate a book idea

2) Research your book

3) Outline your book

4) Write each chapter

Meeting the Writer's Deadline examines how to manage a book project, so the author accomplishes individual tasks by the delivery date, regardless of whether that due date is set by a traditional publisher, a book bundle editor, or is self-imposed. If you struggle with finishing work by a deadline you might find the book helpful.

When you are writing a book, you will encounter dependent tasks. A dependent task cannot start until another to-do item ends. If there are only two or three dependent tasks, you might handle them the way you handle your other to-do list items, taking care to schedule them in the order required. If you have more than three dependent tasks, recognize that you have a project and treat the to-dos as a group.

TIP: Business Books for Writers resources page provides info on managing projects

The Resources page at Business Books for Writers

www.businessbooksforwriters.com/resources

has information and links to articles on managing projects. Another great resource for learning more about managing projects is the monthly *Writing Entrepreneur* newsletter.

www.BusinessBooksforWriters.com/ TheWritingEntrepreneur

Choosing tasks to complete for the week

Step 1: Choose the fifteen tasks you want to complete during the coming week (three tasks for each workday).

Step 2: Start with any action items that must be completed on Monday.

Do not select more than three to-do items for Monday.

If you do not have three tasks to work on yet, go to the "Not Important and Urgent" quadrant and select an item that you can't delete to complete your list of three to-dos for Monday. If you have no items in the category, then check your "Important and Not Urgent" list.

Sort the remaining twelve items using the same strategy assigning three to-do's for each day of the week.

Any new or incoming to-do items that must be completed immediately during the day should go into the "Important and Urgent" quadrant. You might even have to work on them the same day you get them. This often happens. When this occurs, move the tasks you cannot finish to another day.

Remember, completing three tasks a day is a goal. If you don't hit the goal, don't despair. The system is designed to help you remember to-do tasks and not forget them. Sometimes the timing of when you complete action items is out of your control.

Update the quadrant at the end of the week with any tasks you did not complete during the week. Include action items from the master list with due dates for the week. Again, don't put more than fifteen action items on your weekly list.

5.10 Develop your way of organizing your to-do list

Ask successful authors how they handle their to-do lists, and you will get almost as many answers as the number of writers you ask. Everyone has his or her way of handling his or her action list. If you ask most writers who have used a system for managing their task list if they have always used the same system they employ today, they will probably answer, no! It is very common for successful authors to keep looking for new and better ways to improve their efficiency.

In part, this is true because the writers are getting better at being more efficient. Over time, they are getting more done because they have learned to organize and complete their list in a way that works well for them. Most of us find that just as we think we have this to-do list thing conquered, we find some aspect of it isn't working for us anymore; or, most likely, we learn about a new tool or new approach that makes us even *more* efficient than the process we used before.

Therefore, this book doesn't try to tell you exactly how to create a to-do list process that will always work for you.

Instead, several approaches are discussed. Once you are comfortable with the process, don't be afraid to modify the method covered, or to experiment. The fundamentals will remain the same.

Chapter 5 Points to remember

1) Keep your process as simple as you can.

2) Remember the Rule of Three.

3) The Eisenhower Quadrant is a useful method for determining how to prioritize your to-do list.

Next Step: Managing documents

Often a task produces documentation that you may need in the future to complete other projects that arise. You will have more time to do your work if you can quickly find these materials.

PART 4: TO-DO LIST MANAGEMENT SYSTEM

Chapter 6: Document Management With Evernote

Record-keeping sounds boring, but if you want to get things done as a writer and indie publisher, you have to know where to find the stuff you have done, your contracts, reports, plans, financial records, etc. In other words, you need a record management system.

There are a lot of record management systems available as cloud-based applications, but most of them are complicated, with more features than writers need. These applications can also be expensive.

You can set up your record keeping system in an email program such as Outlook, in Scrivener, or in many other programs; but many writers agree that Evernote and Scrivener are a great combination. If you use Outlook, you may already have OneNote. OneNote and Evernote are very similar. If you have One Note and are comfortable using it, then there is no reason for you to switch to Evernote.

Scrivener is great for managing your research notes, in part because you can import web pages. When the web page is updated, the page content you have saved within Scrivener automatically updates as well. Another nice research feature of Scrivener is the ability to create cards, which you can move around as if you were rearranging a bunch of physical note cards on your desk, but Scrivener is not useful as a document management tool as some other options because you cannot create notebooks in Scrivener and you cannot email documents into Scrivener. The search capability within and across files is limited in Scrivener compared to Evernote or One Note. For this reason, I use both Scrivener (where I keep all the research, notes, outline, photos, etc., on a writing project) and Evernote. I then create a note in Evernote with the Scrivener file as an attachment. The Scrivener file is stored as a compressed file.

You might ask why I bother doing this when I can just store the Scrivener file on my computer. Storing the file in Evernote means I have one place to go to find all my documents related to a book. I can store my excel revenue and cost sheets in Evernote, my testimonials, my cover jpgs, etc. And Evernote has a great search that allows me to easily find information based on a few words. You can also do a search on your hand written notes that you have scanned into your Evernote program. If the file is stored on the computer, I need to know the file name or use a tag system.

The limitation of Scrivener as a document management system is that each project requires a different Scrivener file.

Chapter 6: Document Management With Evernote

Nick Hacker wrote a blog post that shows how he uses Scrivener and Evernote together when he writes a novel. You can read his article, "Using Scrivener and Evernote to Write Your Book"[10].

Evernote allows you to stack notebooks — putting one into another as if you were putting manila folders into hanging folders in a physical filing system.

Another approach to using Evernote is to create one notebook and use tags to identify all the files. You can do this whether you use one notebook or numerous notebooks.

Establishing a tagging system creates a powerful way to search and locate documents. You can easily see the tags in a directory. To find a note you just click on the tag name to see the notes assigned to that label.

There are many books written about using Evernote, but the key to success is setting up a consistent system.

6.1 Evernote for writers

When I first started using Evernote, I created a notebook for everything. I put notebooks inside notebooks, because, well, I could. But I soon discovered that having so many made finding information more difficult. Here are the ones I recommend:

- Inbox – Evernote comes with the Inbox notebook already set up for you. Don't delete it. This notebook is where Evernote stores email you forward to yourself when you do not designate a notebook name or use tag(s).

- Appointments – Keep all your appointments in one notebook. Evernote has a reminder function. You can integrate an Evernote reminder with Microsoft's Outlook app calendar, although most authors with Outlook use Microsoft's One Note rather than Evernote.

- Shared – Store notes that you have shared with someone else. These might be notes you have sent to yourself, or a copy of an email indicating that you have done your part of a book project and are waiting for a reply from another author. Writers use shared notebooks to keep manuscripts attached to an email while to track conversations with editors or co-authors.

- Directory – This is where you store notes not listed above.

- Trash – This is where deleted notes go.

This set of notebooks will allow you to organize your record-keeping in Evernote.

6.2 Naming Structure

Create a consistent naming structure. Many writers use a convention similar to the following:

Date: Note_title.content_clue

For example, you might name the note that contains the ISBN you assigned to your latest book:

- Note Name: 2017-04-12: Completing the Writer's To-do List. Print or 2017-04-12: Completing the Writer's To-do List. Ebook
- Note Tags: The tags I would use (remember you can use more than one), would be: ISBN, Completing the Writer's To-do List
- If someone besides me (like an assistant or a spouse) ever needs to find the ISBN for a book in production while you are traveling, they could locate the note in one of two ways:
  o By knowing the date or the title of the book
  o By using the tag (ISBN) or (the name of the book)

Be sure to document your naming structure, so you are always consistent. Evernote keeps a directory of the tag names for you. This is useful because you can click on the Tag name in the directory and pull up all the notes using the tag.

TIP: Create a master list of tags

When using a tagging system, create a master list and use the same tags everywhere — in Evernote, in your to-do app, and in your Pomodoro app. That way you will start to remember the labels you use most often and save time.

6.3 Schedule an administrative day

It is easy to get behind on record-keeping. This is one task that often drops to the bottom of people's to-do list. However, if you stay on top of your financial record-keeping throughout the year, you will experience a lot less stress at tax time — and get your refund back sooner.

6.4 If you hate record-keeping

If you hate record-keeping, look into getting a personal assistant or a virtual assistant to handle some of your administrative tasks, such as simple website updates.

A local high school student who wanted a career as a writer approached a novelist and asked if the author could use an intern. They agreed on a set salary for the summer that fit within the writer's budget and the intern updated the resource page of the author's website and similar administrative work.

Another writer hired a personal assistant through the Internet to do their electronic record organization once a week. Over time this virtual assistant also took over additional marketing tasks under the direction of the author, such as calendar scheduling, etc.

TIP: Never let anyone else handle your financial record-keeping

- Never let anyone else handle your finances.
- Don't give anyone else access to your checks.
- Don't give anyone else the password to your online bank accounts.
- Don't give anyone else your credit card information.

Allowing other people to have access to your financial information invites them to steal your money. Bookkeepers steal money. Lawyers steal money. Assistants, virtual or otherwise, steal money. If people don't have access to your finances, they can't steal your money.

Chapter 6 Points to remember

1) Set up a record-keeping system so you can find information quickly and easily.

2) Learn to use tags/labels to simplify your record-keeping system.

3) Never outsource the handling of your finances to anyone else.

Next Step: Making the process a habit

In the next chapter we will discuss briefly how to develop the habit of following your process on a daily basis over an 8-week period.

Chapter 7: Staying With The Program

For many writers, following a program where you write down what you want to accomplish each day requires a shift in their daily routine. Taking the time each week to figure out what are the most important tasks you want to accomplish in the coming week is something they haven't tried before.

Setting aside time each week for administrative tasks may sound nice in theory, but when you are working full-time at the job that puts food on the table, the only time you have to do administrative tasks is in the evening after work or on the weekend — the same time when you can finally sit down and write!

You have to believe the benefits of completing three to-do items every day are going to help you realize your writing dreams. And then you have to remember you were convinced this shift in approach would help you! Remembering can be hard, especially when you first start out. You may have the best of intentions of finally following a process to stay up-to-date with all the things you must do, have been asked to do, and want to do; but it is hard to stick with a program that requires a change in your daily routine. If you have made it this far into this book, then I'm sure you want to get more done with your writing, but how do you stay with the program?

7.1 Habits

You may hear or read that conventional wisdom says that it takes three weeks to form a habit. At the end of three weeks, you will start to remember that you should be doing that new task or routine you want to adopt, but it takes around eight weeks for you to adjust to this new routine and to feel odd if something comes up that prevents you from doing your routine.

In his online article, James Clear discusses how the three-week myth entered our culture and reviews research that shows it takes much longer than most people think to change behavior. "How Long Does It Actually Take to Form a New Habit? (Backed by Science)." [11]

If you develop a schedule that you can stick to, you will be able to follow your to-do list process. If you execute your program every workday for three weeks, then you will be well on your way to the point where you have internalized the discipline to complete your three action items consistently.

Those eight weeks might be tough, although, after the first three weeks, they will get increasingly easier. When you first begin setting aside a specific time for writing down three to-do items at the end of each day, it will be hard. You are tired at the end of the workday, especially if you also have a day job. You will be tempted to put off assigning tasks until the next morning. Then, instead of starting your tasks first thing, you will take up time debating what tasks to do.

Most people have no problem the first day they check their to-do list at their desk, but they often forget the next day.

If you do well the first few days and then get busy and forget, don't despair. You created a schedule and the routine you want to develop. You have a plan to record your three to-do items each day, and you know if you don't finish all three goals, you will move the unfinished to-dos to the next day. There will probably be days during those three weeks when you forget to write down your three to-do list items for the day. There will be times when urgent matters take over your day, and you don't get even one of your three goals completed.

When you don't accomplish what you planned, don't beat up on yourself. Everyone struggles with following their schedule from time to time. The issue is not can you follow your plan but when something prevents you from following your process, but do you know how to resume your schedule the next day? Use the plan and remember, you are making a lifestyle change. Expect some setbacks. You aren't failing when you don't fallow the plan one day, you are adjusting to a new way of managing your time.

7.2 Stick to your lifestyle change

To stick with your to-do list process over time, you need to remember the pain you experienced when you had no plan. Remember the embarrassment of forgetting an important task you promised another writer or an editor. Remember the promise you made to yourself that you would learn to get on top of your to-do list. Remember the reason you bought this book.

Motivate yourself by writing down the benefits you are getting from completing your to-do list and finishing those tasks you want to get done each day. Everyone will have their unique list. My benefits list consists of:

1) I have a reputation of being someone who, when they say they will get something done, they meet their deadline.

2) I no longer spend time on less urgent tasks that I happen to remember, and then, at the end of the day (when it is too late), realize I missed today's deadline.

3) I no longer wake up in the middle of the night remembering something I promised to do but had forgotten, and then can't go back to sleep for hours as I toss and turn and worry about how I'm going to apologize the next day for letting someone down.

There are other benefits to completing my to-do list each day, but one reason the rule of three works so well is that, when you limit your list to three items, you are more liable to remember them.

Mystery writers use this concept all the time — they know that if they want to bury clues in a list that contains four or more items few readers will notice, or remember, the clue in the middle of the list. At the end of the book when the reader learns who did the crime, they realize the clue was stated at the beginning of the story. Action items buried in the middle of a long list also get forgotten!

7.3 An eight-week program for developing a habit

Week 1

During the first week, look for anything in your process that you find challenging. It may be helpful to create a flowchart to help you visualize the steps you intend to take. You can download an example flowchart for a writer's to-do process at **bit.ly/2wMSXA2.**

TIP: Use reminders

Set a reminder on your watch, mobile device, laptop, or desktop for the time when you are supposed to start working on your MIT (Most Important Task).

Completing your MIT will give you the boost in confidence that will help you remember and tackle the remaining two to-dos for the first day.

At the end of the week use the Eisenhower Quadrant to identify the fifteen to-dos tasks you want to complete for the upcoming week. Assign three of these tasks to the next business day.

Week 2

If you make it through Week 1 and finish your three to-do's every day, then CONGRATULATIONS! You are doing great. Keep working through your to-do list. At the end of the second week, you will have completed about thirty items. A few of these will have come in during the week from voicemails or email, or maybe even through networking. That still means you have probably tackled a chunk of that long to-do list you created in Chapter 3.

You may have started to think of adjustments you want to make to the process to make the schedule or the approach easier for you. Go ahead and make those changes — just be sure not to make your system more complicated. The fact the process is simple is the reason you are sticking with it and completing those to-do items.

Week 3

You are on the home stretch regarding developing the habit of following your to-do schedule and process. By now, you should find choosing three to-dos in the evening for the next day is much easier to remember.

You have adjusted and uncovered a schedule that allows you to check your voicemail and email during the day, and are comfortable organizing all email and tasks that come to you.

By the end of the third week, you should see the benefits of following a to-do list process. You have completed about forty-five to-do tasks. You may have even completed all of the to-do items on the original list you compiled when you first started reading this book.

Week 4

As you go through week 4, you should find that your confidence in your ability to handle to-do items is growing. You may occasionally forget to write down your to-do items, but chances are you remember your lapse at the end of the day. More often than not though, you are following your plan.

Week 5-8

You will become more comfortable with your new routine during the next three weeks. There will be times when you realize at the end of your writing time that you forgot to check your to-do list at the start of your writing day. But somewhere around day 66, you will realize that you rarely have to remind yourself to check your to-do list at the outset of the day, and you typically write down your three to-do items for the next day at the end of your working day. When that day happens, you will know you are now in the habit of following your process.

7.4 When you get behind

Life has a way of interrupting our well-meaning plans. At some point, you will get sick, or go on vacation, or need to concentrate on family issues that take up the time you were spending maintaining your to-do list and completing those tasks.

Expect these things to happen. I have studied with the writers and publishers, Dean Wesley Smith and Kristine Rusch for many years, and they have a term for events that impact your writing productivity and your indie publishing plans. They call such setbacks "life rolls."

We all have experienced circumstances that require our attention. Do not be surprised when these "life rolls" occur. Instead, have a strategy already in place for dealing with them.

First, contact anyone who might be affected by your inability to complete a to-do list item by its due date. You do not need to discuss private matters you would rather keep to yourself, just inform them you need to deal with personal issues. Propose a revised delivery date. No one should get upset with you for having to deal with unforeseen situations.

People get upset when you repeatedly ask for new deadlines or miss a deadline and never contact them to let them know you will not be turning something in on time. One of the advantages of having a system for handling your to-do list is that you are delivering on a consistent basis, so a constant inability to meet deadlines should no longer be an issue (if it was before).

Many of your to-do list items will be tasks you set for yourself and your writing business. Don't worry; your to-do list will still be there waiting for you when you can start working on it again.

Oh, sure, you will be behind schedule, just like you were when you started this book. Many indie publishers get frustrated when they don't finish their to-do list according to plan. They throw up their hands and abandon their to-do list process. *Don't do that!*

Just reopen this book, work your way through Chapter 3, and capture all those to-do items again. Once you have a single, master list of the to-do items that built up during your life roll, go through them using the "Do-in-under-2-minutes, delete, delegate, or defer" approach. Go back to your Administrative day, knowing it may take a few weeks to catch up on your filing. Your business will survive and be better off if you return to process — although you might need to reestablish your habit of following your process!

Chapter 7 Points to remember

1) Integrating your to-do list process into your schedule will require you to develop new habits.

2) You will get discouraged, but if you find you have stopped following your process, you can always go back and start using your plan again.

3) If you do need to start over, pull out this book and make modifications based on your experience and start using a task list again.

Next Step: Dealing with distractions

Some days you are enjoying your work so much that completing your projects is easy. Other days though, distractions can waste a great deal of time. In the next chapter, we will take a look at how to deal with distractions and get you back to work on the activities that matter most to your success.

Chapter 8:
How To Deal With Distractions

A key to completing what you have to do is to avoid what you do not need to do. This advice sounds simple, but can be difficult to implement. Just as we created a process for completing our to-do tasks, you need a method of ignoring distractions. Let's look at five ways to staying focused on your work:

1) Determine what actions to work on and their priority

2) Monitor your ability to stay focused

3) Learn to recognize when you are distracted

4) Develop a method for resetting your attention

5) Recognize your success no matter how small

8.1 Determine what actions to work on and their priority

Everyone has an extensive list of things they want to do. Many people add goals, objectives, and strategies to their to-do list. These are not to-do items. They are tools that help you determine what you want to achieve and how you plan to succeed. Each of these tools belongs to your writer's business plan, where you can revisit and revise them as you learn more about your business, your audience, and your marketplace. Only *tasks* should be on your to-do list.

Let's take a look at how supporting the sections of your business plan with your task list, lead to your success.

Goals: Your business plan starts with identifying your goals for your business. The first thing you want to do is identify what you want to achieve.

Example: I want to write four novels during the first year of writing full-time.

Strategy: *How* you are going to achieve your goal? I will set up a schedule so that I write a novel in one month, edit a novel in one month and submit a novel to my agent every three months.

Objectives: Measurable and specific steps you are going to take to achieve your strategy. I am going to use social media to increase my mailing list by 15% each year to reach 5000 subscribers by 2020.

Tactics: Actions you are going to take to achieve your objectives. I will use blogging, follow-backs, and ads to grow my Twitter following to 5000 followers my first year, 10000 followers the second year and 20000 followers during my third year of business.

To-Do items: Specific tasks that must be done to complete your tactics. Examples would be:

1) I will distribute a free ebook to my website as a way of collecting email addresses so I can communicate to my readers.

2) I will write a customized Thank You direct message for my twitter followers.

3) I will include a link to my signup form for my free ebook.

4) I will create a web page signup form for Twitter followers who click on my web link.

Even after you go through your master to-do list and remove any goals, strategy statements, objectives and tactics, you will still have many tasks on your list because you are growing a business. You will always have more things to do than time to do them.

Don't overwhelm yourself with action items. Choose the three items you most need to get done each day. Schedule the time on your calendar when you will work on each of your three to-do tasks. This time can vary each day. Use a reminder alert to avoid forgetting a task.

Do not worry if you are unable to complete the to-do item in the amount of time you assign to the job. That is okay. If you do not finish, schedule time the next day to continue work. You will eventually complete the to-do item. Tasks that don't get done are tasks with no assigned work time and no deadline.

When you receive a task that you must complete the same day it is assigned, your previously planned action items may need to be delayed. If you find yourself in this position, review the due dates of postponed items to develop a schedule that allows you to complete the work by deadline. If you have items with strict due dates this approach might require a few longer workdays.

Another option for adjusting to unanticipated items that must be completed at once is to examine the priority of tasks you have assigned yourself. Think about the difference between tasks you have to do and those you want to do. The former has the higher priority, but don't keep lowering the priority of those you give yourself, or you may never get them done.

If you take more than two days to complete a to-do item, think about whether you can break the task into smaller portions. If you can divide a task into a checklist of work, you are working on a project, not an individual task. Smaller tasks are not as intimidating as projects.

Breaking tasks down into more manageable parts reduces the temptation to procrastinate. When you divide a to-do, remember that you are adding tasks to your list. Record the new to-do items, estimate the time to complete them and schedule a time to complete them. Since you only list three to-do's per day, move the other to-dos to another day.

Studies have shown that are better at remembering action items when they physically write tasks on paper. As stated in Chapter 1, putting a sticky note on your monitor also helps you to remember to start working on your list.

TIP: If you need extra time to complete your task you haven't failed!

People sometimes feel like they are not productive when they don't finish three tasks in one day. Some to-dos take more than one day to complete. Determine at the end of each workday which to-dos you will work on the next day as part of your process. List the unfinished task as your first task for the next day. As long as you remember to work on your task during the designated time without wasting time with non-task related distractions, you are succeeding in managing your to-do list.

8.2 Monitor your ability to stay focused

When your mind wanders from your work, you often don't realize you have been distracted. To stay focused on your task you need to train yourself to recognize when you are distracted and develop a method to refocus your attention.

Zoe B. (her last name is never listed), in her online article, "8 ways to Reduce Distractions"[12] **https://simplelifestrategies.com/sls-reduce-distractions** recommends before you start on a task that you tell yourself you are going to focus on your to-do item for a specific amount of time. When you take this approach, you can prepare mentally to stay on task.

Pomodoro Timers

A Pomodoro timer is so helpful when you struggle to remain focused because you can only be distracted for the length of one work cycle. The Pomodoro approach has you set a timer to work 25 minutes and then take a five-minute break. You might be distracted as much as 25 minutes, but when the timer goes off, you realize you are no longer working on your task. After your five-minute break, you can start working again. When you first start working with a Pomodoro timer, you may find yourself checking to see how much time is left until your break. (The amount of time left can be set to appear in your menu.) Rather than look at how much longer you must work, look at it as the amount of time until you can reward yourself with a break. Chapter 8 in *Meeting The Writers Deadline* has a section on using a Pomodoro timer. You can also information on Pomodoro timers on the Tools page of the Business Books For Writers website, **www.businessbooksforwriters.com/tools/**

At the end of this chapter you will find two Pomodoro timer applications you can use to let you know when to stop for breaks and to time your work sessions.

Use your breaks to recapture your energy

Be careful to stick to your five-minute break. Mail, Facebook, Amazon sales, etc., can all seduce you into forgetting to resume your writing while on your break. Some authors schedule a block of time twice a day for social media marketing. Try using your five-minute break for activities that will help your concentration during your next Pomodoro cycle, such as jumping jacks, fixing a cup of tea or five minutes of meditation.

Starting Tasks

If you have trouble starting a task take a minute to review why you are spending your time on the to-do item. You are spending time and money investing in your writing career. You want your business to succeed because, if you finish and successfully sell your books, you will earn the money that can lead to reaching your goals for your life, your family, and your business. You can achieve the full-time writing career you want. You can help your family. You can establish the type of life you want because you control how you spend your time.

When you are tired, take time to re-energize

Writing takes a physical toll on you. Sometimes, I become so tired and quit trying to work and take a thirty-minute nap instead. According to Mark Ehrman and Sara Mednick in their book *Take a Nap! Change Your Life* [12], you need sleep to be productive. You can't write well when you struggle to keep your eyes open. You also can't enjoy your work when you are sleepy. One nice thing about the Pomodoro timer I use, Be Focused Pro, is the pause feature. Whenever I'm too tired to continue working, I put my timer on pause and take a nap, then continue my work when I wake up!

8.3 Plan your work around your most productive time

You need to know the time each day when you can concentrate best. When you work full-time as a writer, you can write when you are most productive. Not everyone has that option. During my high-tech career days, I didn't have a choice as to when I worked on my writing to-do list. I wrote during my hour commute to and from the office.

When I started writing full-time, I tried to follow the same routine as I used during my high tech work day. I went to bed at 11 pm, got up at 6 am, had breakfast, exercised since I no longer had an hour train ride, wrote from 8 until noon. I planned to do business tasks from one until five when I broke for dinner. Then read from 7 pm until 9 pm.

I found I could I could never settle down and start writing until 10 am. From 10 am until 5 pm, I can focus on my writing and ignore disruptions so I altered my schedule. I started doing business tasks from 8 am until 10 am, then start my writing.

Everyone is different. If you are just starting to write full-time, coming up with a schedule can be a challenge. Don't be afraid to make changes to your schedule. Identify your most productive work time and adjust your schedule to accomplish your writing (which always gets first priority) and then your task list.

I found I like doing the things that tend to distract me the most during the day like emails, phone calls, and marketing work from 8-10 am. Once I have these tasks out of the way I can concentrate on my writing. Okay, I do take 30-60 minutes for lunch!

8.4 Meet your deadline

Even if you are working at home, you need to assign a deadline to each to-do item. Consistently hitting your due dates drives your business forward. When you find yourself working on distracting activities, you are spending time on something that will not help you reach your writing business goals. The author and writing teacher, Dean Wesley Smith, tells his students: "You are in charge of your own career." Take responsibility for your success or failure by deciding that the way you will achieve your goal of a full-time writing career is to complete the tasks required to be successful.

Make a conscious decision you will start and finish your to-do items. If you find yourself spending time on things that will not help your business succeed you need to stop yourself and asked, will this activity help me reach my writing career goals? Reading about the latest political poll probably won't help you finish your latest book or hit your revenue goals.

8.5 Develop a method for resetting your attention

You realize you are working on something other than the to-do list you were determined to complete. What do you do? Learn to recognize you have become distracted. Stop. Reset your attention and go back to the task you listed to be completed.

Eliminate distractions that repeatedly keep you from working on what you need to accomplish. If you find yourself surfing the Internet when you are supposed to be writing, turn off your Wi-Fi connection. I know how it goes. We all so. You are writing and then find you need to do some research. Instead of going on the Internet and doing the research right then, try making a note in your document that you need to look something up, such as "verify Bern, Switzerland's medieval town clock is next to the bear fountain." Then continue writing. You can search later for the square brackets you inserted to find those places where you need to do Internet research. Make "research my novel" a separate to-do item.

You can also turn on the "Focus View" option in MS Word or the "Full Screen" option in Scrivener or the equivalent in your word processing program to avoid being sidetracked by computer distractions. When you can't easily see your email icon or your browser icon, you may experience an easier time concentrating on your work.

If you repeatedly get distracted, take a break and write down all the things you will NOT do during your task time, such as surfing the internet or reading email newsletters.

8.6 Protect your writing business time

Do you have friends who "drop by" to say hello? I grew up in rural Ohio, and this was a common occurrence. When you work at home, such pop in visits can torpedo work progress. If people telephone ahead before coming by, let them know you are working and suggest a more convenient time. Perhaps they could visit after your workday is over, if you write full-time, or set aside a day in your schedule for visits. If they do show up unannounced, then let them know you will have to go back to work in a half hour. This way you sacrifice one writing period and break to spend time with friends.

I have found that my friends respect the fact that I work at home. When I explain I work an 8 to 5 pm workday but want to spend time with them, they tend to schedule get together rather than drop by. One you get a few books published, your friends will start to think of your writing as an occupation not a hobby. It does get easier.

Never put work ahead of a family member or friend in need, though. If a friend needs you, remember, you can always catch up your task later. You can also schedule time to your to-do items when people most likely to interrupt you are not around.

Use voice mail

If phone calls keep interrupting you, turn off your phone's ringer and let calls go to voicemail.

If someone needs to reach you, they will leave a voicemail, and you can decide if you need to call them right back or return their call later.

Turn off notifications

Beware of notifications generated by your email program, apps, etc. They can sabotage your concentration and distract you. If you find yourself distracted by such interruptions, turn notifications off! (On a Mac you can turn them off by clicking on System Preferences -> Notifications. You can find out how to turn off notifications on phones and other computers by doing a browser search for "How do you turn off notifications?" Turning off the notification option is today's equivalent of unplugging the old landline phone cable).

Block out sounds

Do you live in the middle of a big city? Chances are your brain already ignores the noise, but, if noise is an issue, I discovered by accident that the noise canceling headphones I use on a plane also work when I'm not listening to music. Joanna Penn mentions on her website that she also uses noise-cancelling headphones (the same Bose headphones my husband gave me for my birthday one year)! **www.thecreativepenn.com**

Don't know why you get so distracted when you try to settle down to work? Maybe your writing environment is distracting. Try cleaning your workspace. Take everything off your messy desk, dump them into a box, set the box in another room, and try writing. When you are done put the items away, throw them out or give them away.

Environment

Some authors find they can't write in the same room in which they do non-writing or business tasks. When they do creative work in the room they use for business they find themselves thinking about the upcoming hosting bill rather than their cute meet in their romance story. If they are working on their taxes in the room where they have spent years solving true crime stories, they discover their thoughts revert to police procedures rather than deductions. If you find your setting causing issues for you, set up a separate space to write.

Noise can be good

Maybe you need more activity around you to settle down and concentrate. Authors who need more stimulation go to coffee houses to sit down and write. A compromise can be to work in a library if you want some activity around but minimal noise.

Tip: Identify your distraction

When you find you have an ongoing problem focusing on your work, experiment to find how to identify, and then eliminate, the distraction.

8.7 Procrastination

Maybe the issue that prevents you from work is not distractions but starting to work. Often writers stall because the task they want to accomplish is overwhelming. How do you write an entire book series? The answer, of course, is you write one paragraph at a time until you finish a book and then you do the same for each book in the series. If you struggle to start, you might do better by breaking an intimidating task into smaller tasks.

Don't be afraid to adjust your to-do list goals even after you have started on a task. For example, you might decide to divide a task into smaller components. Recognize each task is now a separate to-do item. Determine if one task must be done before the next can begin. Readjust your three goals for the day. Move any more than three goals to the next day, sticking with your three-goal per day limit.

Don't hesitate to put a task on hold if you hit a roadblock and can't proceed until you complete unanticipated work. Follow the same approach as in the previous paragraph. Identify this extra work as a task. Give it a deadline. Schedule the work. Make it one of your three tasks for the day and start to work.

When you have finished, move the task you put on hold up to be the next to-do item on your list and complete that task. Over time you will become good at recognizing when you need to break a to-do item into smaller tasks.

8.8 You won't make your deadline every day

What do you do when you can't complete one task, let alone three in one day? First, don't get discouraged. You will always have those days when you don't finish anything, let alone all three to-do items. The purpose of your to-do process is to make sure you don't forget to work on your tasks. As long as you have a plan for completing the work you need to finish by deadline, you will complete all your tasks eventually, even if you need more time to do so than you predicted.

Be realistic. If one of your tasks will require several days to complete, then allocate those days to the task. Adjust your schedule, as you need to complete your work.

I still like to complete three tasks in one day. When I have a big task that cannot be broken down into smaller tasks but will require several days, I will add two small tasks to the day and do those first, so that I complete the bigger task over the course of the week.

You might ask doesn't this violate the "do the Most Important Task first" advice? The answer is yes. That is why I say you need to be flexible. Use common sense when it comes to how to complete your tasks. If you have a small task that must be completed, then that can become your most important task. The most important task to complete does not always have to be the item that will take the most time to be completed.

Assign a top priority for to-do deadlines set by others. Your professional reputation is important when building a business. You do not want to turn work in late. Before you agree to any outside work, review your current due dates to verify you can complete the work in time.

The time to ask for additional time is when someone asks you to do a task, not after you have agreed to do the work. The other person can decide whether to ask someone else to help out or to reset their timeline to accommodate your schedule. (Remember I'm talking about your writing tasks. This doesn't work well in a corporate environment when you boss asks you to do a task!)

Avoid agreeing to do two tasks that share a deadline. You can find yourself struggling to finish both and risk completing neither on time. When the second request comes in, no matter how much bigger the opportunity might be if you agree to the task, you must decide if you can make your first commitment before saying you will undertake the second task. You can ask for more time for the second task, but do not blow off the first. The publishing world is small, and word will get around if you miss a deadline. You will not suffer any consequences if you ask for more time. Instead, you will establish a reputation for taking deadlines seriously.

8.9 Recognize your success no matter how small

When you are trying to change your habits, take care how you define a setback. In the beginning, if you organize a to-do list and start working on a to-do item, you have had a degree of success. If you finish one to-do, you have succeeded. If you finish two or three, you have accomplished a lot.

Your goal is to finish three goals a day, but you are making progress if you only complete one a day, because that adds up to 365 tasks a year. If you stay focused and have a bit of luck, you may find yourself finishing three tasks a day or 1095 each year. You will be much further ahead if you get three to-dos done every day than if you sit and worry about the fact that you never find the time to complete a to-do item.

Once you start hitting your goals consistently, you will find completing your daily to-do list gets easier. Success almost always follows success.

8.10 Tools

Every Business Book for Writers has included a list of tools related to the theme of the book. Tools help you work more efficiently, and they can aid in organization.

However, new tools continue to hit the market. Use your judgment regarding whether to try one of the listed applications. They are included to make you aware such tools exist.

Many writers do not use any aids at all. Sometimes you go through several before you find the tools that work best for you, so don't be afraid to try them and don't be afraid to quit using them if they do not make you more efficient. You will find more tools on the Business Books for Writers Resource page.

Since prices are subject to change, I have not listed the prices for each of these products. Many companies offer a free and a pro version. Instead of listing the cost of each application I have provided a link to the online page where you can get pricing information. None of these applications are expensive.

8.11 Tools that help you focus

Pomodoro Timers

- Be Focused Pro – Focus Timer & Goal Tracker By Denys Yevenko. Mac, IOS app.

I use Be Focused Pro for my Pomodoro timer. It is one of the most popular Apple apps for helping you time writing sprints and breaks.

- FocusBooster (Mac and PC) **www.focusboosterapp.com/download**.

FocusBooster also is a Pomodoro application that you can use not just to keep you focused, but also to track the amount of time you are working. You can assign a value to your time and use this app to calculate hourly charges for clients.

8.12 Apps that eliminate distractions

I turn on the Focus View option of MS Word when I write to avoid being distracted by anything else on my screen, and of course, I turn off "Notifications." However, some writers prefer more help in ignoring screen distractions. The following apps are some of the more popular services used by authors, but more are available. A longer list is included in your downloads file:

www.BusinessBooksForWriters.com/ctwtdl-links

FocusWriter. Linux, Windows, and Mac OS X

FocusWriter is a simple, distraction-free writing environment. You access features by moving your mouse to the edges of the screen, so even the program doesn't distract you! You can get FocusWriter in a variety of languages.

Anti-Social

This app has been renamed Freedom. Mac OS X 10.8 – 10.12; Windows Vista, 7, 8, 10; iOS 9+ (iPad, iPhone)

Freedom is designed to allow you to block Internet sites that typically distract you such as Facebook, Instagram, Twitter, LinkedIn, etc. You can also block the internet altogether. Of course, you can do this by turning off your connection to Wi-Fi as well. If you need to access some sites, Freedom might be an inexpensive way to keep you off the most tempting sites that you do not need access to while writing or working on your to-dos. You can also schedule sessions and can choose to have them start automatically.

Chapter 8 Points to remember

1) You will make more progress on your task list if you avoid spending time on tasks you do not need to do.

2) Schedule three tasks each day and don't be discouraged if you are not able to complete all three. Some to-dos take longer than we think. Move the uncompleted tasks to the next day.

3) Teach yourself to recognize when you are being distracted and devise a method of getting yourself back on track.

Next Step: Track what you have completed

Keeping your email list under control is as important as managing your To-Do list. Get tips on staying current with your email in the next chapter.

Chapter 9:
Email – The Great
Time Sink

In Chapter three, you created a master list of action items that needed to be completed by going through your email list. You may still have a lot of emails in your Inbox.

If you have a good email processing system and have no lurking tasks in your email Inbox or your mail folders, then you can skip this section.

9.1 Follow a system and you can keep up with your emails

You need a system for keeping up with your emails. If you have hundreds or thousands of emails in your Inbox you will lose track of information you need and quite possibly forget tasks contained in emails. Productivity experts talk about creating a system for "getting your Inbox down to zero." Recognize this is an impossible goal. As soon as our email Inbox hits zero, inevitably a new message arrives! So while an Inbox with zero messages is a goal, it is a momentary achievement.

Author Brigid Schulte describes in her Washington Post article[13] from August 12, 2014, "In two weeks, I went from 23,768 e-mails in my Inbox to zero. Here's how." she writes that she learned to handle her email from Julie Gray, a time coach who helps people who are overwhelmed with email. Julie said the first thing Brigid had to do was recognize that the problem wasn't Brigid was doing something wrong. "This is such a pervasive problem. People think, 'what am I doing wrong?' They think they don't have discipline or focus or that there's some huge character flaw and they're beating themselves up all the time. Which only makes it worse."

Julie had to change her e-mail mindset and understand that the issue wasn't she was a failure or couldn't learn to manage her emails; the problem was she had no system for processing her emails.

Just like you need a system to follow to keep up with all the tasks you need to complete as an author, you need a system to be on top of all the emails you get.

You might ask why discuss how to control your email in a book on how to complete your to-do list? Emails are the main time sink and distraction for many writers. We love to read. We love to learn about new things. We love to ask ourselves, what if? Naturally, we are just the type of creative who thinks of every email as another little nugget we might use in a story.

If you learn to control your use of email and handling of emails, you will create more time to complete your action items. Use the advice in this section and the time you create for working as opposed to reading emails will greatly increase.

If your Inbox has thousands of unread emails and you have no idea whether you have tasks in those emails you should work on or not, then you need to keep reading. Bite the bullet and take the time to sort through your messages. Once you clean out and organize your email, you will be set to capture all the action items that come to your email.

Sorting through your email will take a while, but in the end, completing the day with your email under control reduces your stress.

Email Inboxes often contain the bulk of our hidden to-do items.

9.2 Get your email under control

At one point, I had over 55,000 unopened emails. I check my email three times a day to look for important messages — but with such a backlog it is easy to miss something. For this reason, the first thing we are going to tackle is how to get your email list under control.

When organized our task list we followed David Allen approach of spending no more than 2 minutes evaluating a to-do list item and then taking action by Completing, Deleting, Deferring or Delegating each task. Let's take a look at how to use this idea to conquer your email.

Organize your email backlog

The first thing you want to do as you go through your email backlog is to complete any to-do item that you can finish in two minutes or less. For example, if your task is "let your cover designer know your book's ISBN" send a quick email with the ISBN and move to the next email.

When you encounter an item that requires more than two minutes to complete, add them to your Todoist action item list.

If the email contains information that you signed up to receive such as a newsletter, but are no longer interested in reading, unsubscribe from the newsletter.

This is not hard and can be done in less than two minutes. Almost all emails have an "unsubscribe" button at the bottom of the email. It may be hard to find, but it is usually present in the fine print. Some newsletters make this more difficult than it needs to be and be forewarned, some newsletters won't actually unsubscribe you.

After you have unsubscribed, delete all the emails from the sender.

Tip: Never subscribe to a newsletter with your business email account

I use a Gmail account to collect all the newsletters, general info, etc., that I sign up for rather than have it clog up my business email account. If you have emails in your business email mailbox, consider signing up for them with a free account and unsubscribing from your business email account. You will get fewer incoming emails to your business email account and make it easier to manage.

Move junk email to the junk mail folder.

If the message is something that you enjoy reading when you have free time, such as notifications for blogs you subscribe to, then move those emails to a "Read Later" folder.

TIP: Manage your "read later" emails

Once a year, go through your "Read Later" emails. If you haven't read them by now, chances are you won't read them. Delete any emails more than a year old.

Can you delegate an emailed task to someone else?

Sometimes you must do some work before you can delegate a task. For instance, you might get a request from the person in charge of a writer's conference brochure asking for a different format to the ad you submitted. Forward the email with a comment to your ad designer and delegate the task. If you need to do some work before you can send the email to your ad designer, then move the item to your Todoist list and delegate the remaining tasks later.

Delegate any emails that require work that you typically outsource. For those publishing through a traditional publisher, such tasks might include your bookkeeping, accounting, marketing, social media outreach, etc. Indie publishers could outsource the book production work to a copy editor, proofreader, cover designers, interior book designer, lawyer, accountant, bookkeeper, etc.

When you encounter an action item to delegate, remember only do tasks you can complete in two minutes or less. The temptation is to finish what you need to do and forward the email. Instead, if you cannot complete the task in two minutes, create a reminder in Todoist for later. Avoid the temptation as you go through your email list of getting bogged down by trying to do any task that takes longer than two minutes.

Apply the above process to each email account you use

If you are not in the habit of going through all your email every day, then collecting to-do items from your email list was probably the most time-consuming part of gathering all the steps required to create your master to-do list.

TIP: Create an email address you only use for newsletters, discount offers, etc.

Often when you are doing online research, the site only provides you access if you sign up for their newsletter. Some of these subscriptions you might want to follow, but many you might consider junk mail. By always using the same secondary email address, you can avoid having this "junk" email clutter up your main email account.

Read through the list you compiled earlier of all the places you have stored to-do items. We will now gather items from all the additional places you may have been storing our action items.

Archived emails

You may want to save an email that does not contain an action item. Maybe you have an email exchange between you and a co-author that does not require an action on your part, but you want to retain the information. This type of email is a document that you want to be able to find later. Move them to a new folder labeled "Archived email."

As you go through your email backlog, create an Evernote note, or if you have the Evernote Premium plan, forward the email to your Evernote account whenever you encounter an email you want to retain. For example, a few months after you finish writing your novel you may want to contact, interview, and choose a sound engineer to create an audio version of your book. Set a starting and ending date even if the email fails to specify a timeframe.

9.3 Email hoarders beware

I am an email hoarder. I admit it. I am always afraid that I will delete an email that I need. I confess this trait for two reasons: first, because I know there are many writers are email hoarders, and second, I want to let you know that there is hope for anyone else who suffers from this affliction.

Keeping an email in your Inbox becomes stressful. Every morning you look at the thousands of emails sitting in your Inbox unattended, and you feel like a failure because you haven't the time to keep up with everything. You don't have time to read the emails. You don't have time to answer the emails and you don't have time to determine if you can delete them!

But you can save them!

In Apple Mail, you can use File-> Save As and save an email as an RTF or plain text file. I save the file to the appropriate document folder or I save it to a file called, "Email" on my hard drive.

If you have thousands of emails in your Inbox, you could spend several hours on this task. You can make the job a bit easier if you "flag" the emails that you want to save and delete those you don't. One way to get a start on the project is make cleaning up your emails a to-do task. At the end of the day, all you have to deal with are the flagged emails you want to archive or save in other folders on your hard drive. Remember, to create a new Todoist task for action items you find in your emails.

9.4 Add a day or two to your out of office responder

Most writers use an out of office responder when they go on vacation or travel. Usually, people realize you are not working those days and wait to email you unless they really need to get some information to you. When you use an out of office responder, a good strategy is to set your out of office response to turn off two days after you return from your trip so you have a day to catch up on your email before you start getting your usual volume.

9.5 Do your email offline

Did you ever sit down to go through your email and find that while you are busy on one email several more, just as important emails arrive? Did you stop working on the email you were composing to deal with those and find out later you never finished or sent the first email?

Try doing your email offline. In other words, turn off your Wi-Fi connection. You can read your email when you are not on the Internet. You can reply to the email and hit send. Your email goes into the draft folder. When you turn the Wi-Fi on all the emails you composed automatically are sent!

Use this technique to lower your stress level. Nothing is more stressful than trying to work while more emails keep coming into your Inbox!

9.6 Limit your email accounts

Some writers (especially self-publishers) create multiple email addresses. They have an email address for:

- Their yahoo group
- The author/pen name
- Their family
- Their publishing company
- Their non-fiction pen name

Every email account will attract lots of emails. If you aren't careful instead of two hundred emails a day into one account, you are getting two hundred emails in five or six accounts! Look for ways to limit the number of email accounts you use, and you will have fewer emails.

9.7 SaneBox

One tool that can really cut down on the amount of time you spend going through emails is Sanebox. **www.sanebox.com.** Sanebox puts unimportant emails and newsletters into folders for you. Once a day you get an email listing the emails SaneBox has collected. You then can quickly go through the email list and mark which emails to delete, which to put into your Inbox and which to save to deal with later. Pricing is very reasonable for one account.

If you have several email accounts, as I do, get the lowest price option for Sanebox and use it on the email account that gets the most email. This application really can save you a great amount of time. I have used it for several months and have been very happy.

9.8 View your oldest emails first

Often your email program is set up for you to see your newest emails first. Try putting your oldest emails first and deal with them. This will keep you from going after the newest email and forgetting those that have been patiently waiting for your attention for a while.

Chapter 9 Points to remember

1) You can't manage your to-do list without a system.

2) Apply the Do, Defer, Delegate, Delete technique to your email, just like you did to your to-do list itself.

3) Do your email off-line to avoid the distraction of new emails coming in while you are working on current emails.

Next Step: Track what you have completed

You want to keep a record of the action items you have completed in a Done List. This list will remind you of what you have accomplished which will motivate you to keep with your system, remind you of what worked well so you will repeat your success and help you gauge how you are doing on your year-long goals, so you have time to adjust if necessary.

Chapter 10:
Your Done List!

As was mentioned in Chapter 1, sticky notes serve as great reminders of the most important things to accomplish each day. I attach three sticky note arrows to the monitor where it is easy to see in case I get called away from my desk. When I finish a task, I crumple up the sticky note and throw it away and mark the task "completed" in ToDoist. The program automatically moves the to-do item into a Completed Task or Done List, where all my completed tasks reside.

10.1 Maintain a done list

One crucial step to your success in tracking the work you have finished is to maintain a list of the tasks you have completed. This is called a "Done List." Studies have shown that the key to finishing action items is to remind yourself of all the tasks you have completed.

In their 2011 book, *What motivates you to work hard? The Progress Principle: Using Small Wins to Ignite Joy, Engagement, and Creativity at Work,*[14] Teresa Amabile and Steven Kramer found that a small success increases a person's satisfaction with their work. They describe the reasoning behind this statement. "This pattern is what we call the progress principle: of all the positive events that influence inner work life, the single most powerful is progress in meaningful work; of all the negative events, the single most powerful is the opposite of progress—setbacks in the work. We consider this to be a fundamental management principle: facilitating progress is the most effective way for managers to influence inner work life."

You work harder when you feel that the work you have completed has meaning and others perceive it as done well. It makes sense. As stated earlier you are more successful when you see yourself as having performed successfully. If you feel you are good at what you do, you are going to be more confident you can accomplish what you need to do and more eager to start.

The same idea applies to your task list. When you toil day in and day out on your to-do list, you tend to focus on the tedious hours spent feeling like you will never catch up on all the work you need to do.

Benefits of a Done List

A done list provides more benefits than just motivating you to keep working. Reviewing your Done List provides an opportunity for you to see you have accomplished quite a lot! Reading through everything you finished allows you to see in hindsight how you might handle the task better or faster in the future. You could even discover a way you could have avoided the task altogether, spending your time in a more productive way that would have achieved the same goal.

Small to-do items add up over time, resulting in progress toward achieving your goals. Successful writers need patience when building a fan base or growing revenues. Typically, these things don't happen quickly. Many writers get frustrated when their numbers don't increase each day, but when you review the past several months, you notice your progress. The increases, no matter how small, become encouraging and no longer appear as failures.

The debate: to-do list vs. a done list

Some proponents of Done Lists insist that you don't need a to-do list. Josh Specter in his post for medium.com, "Screw Your To-Do List. You Need A Done List"[15] argues "done lists inspire, to-do lists overwhelm." Proponents of abandoning to-do lists insist that such activity tracking only discourage people and inevitably ends in a person abandoning their attempt to track what they want to do.

Leo Widrith, co-founder of Buffer, believes you need both lists. He wrote a Lifehack article, "Why To-Do Lists Don't Work and Done Lists Do"[16] advocating for using both (although the title wouldn't lead you to think he advocated for using them together.) "The answer isn't to get rid of to-do lists altogether," he claims, "but to remember that a to-do list is the beginning of the journey through Doing to Done."

While there are plenty of authors who argue in favor of using a done list, few believe you should abandon your to-do list.

In his book, *To-Do List Formula: A Stress-Free Guide To Creating To-Do Lists That Work!*[17] Damon Zahariades says that despite the hype around Done Lists, he still thinks the way to achieve progress is to use them.

Decide for yourself that will make you more productive. My biggest problem is remembering to start the most important action I need to work on in the midst of so many things to that need to be completed. A Done list is great for motivating me to keep working when I'm feeling stressed out, but I need a to-do list to organize myself to have items to put on my Done List!

10.2 How to use your done list

There are different strategies for when and how often to review your Done List. Some writers take a quick look at them at the end of each day. I prefer to go over mine at the end of the week. When you first start using your new to-do list process, try doing a quick review at the end of the day, but if you feel that is not efficient, experiment with taking a look at your list at the end of the week, rather than dropping the review altogether.

I also like to review my done list every six months. I have certain financial and strategic goals in my business plan that I revisit every six months, giving me time to adjust if I am behind on hitting my targets. At the end of the year, I check my done list again. Reliving my successes motivates me to strive for bigger goals next year. I get a renewed sense of how I am building on what I have achieved since I started my indie publishing company.

Chapter 10 Points to remember

1) Devise a way to remember to work on your to-do items during the day.

2) Remember Teresa Amabile and Steven Kramer's Progress Principle: You feel better about yourself and your business when you feel you are making progress in your work.

3) A done list reminds you of what you have achieved and inspires you to set bigger goals for you and your writing business.

Next Step: If you quit using your process, just start up again!

Many writers evolve their process for task management over time so the next chapter lists additional books that provide a more in-depth look at this topic.

Chapter 11: It's The Goal That Is Important

A to-do list is a business tool, and you never want to let a tool rule you and your sense of what is important. At some point, you may realize that the goal you set needs to be altered or abandoned. Maybe the economy has changed. Perhaps for the better. An online magazine interview might have raised your sales ten-fold in a week.

The only time you must complete a to-do item is when someone is counting on you to keep your word that you will complete tasks for them.

11.1 Where to find more information on managing your work

I designed Business Books for Writers to be read in a weekend because authors are busy people. Rather than produce a long book that goes into great detail about every aspect of a topic, the books always include links to where you can go to learn more about any aspect of the topic that you would like to explore in depth.

Topics focus on specific skills that indie publishers and writers need to learn, rather than focusing on broad topics that cover a broad overview of how to publish or market a book. Others have already produced great books on those topics.

I have achieved my goal if I leave you wanting to learn even more about managing your tasks after reading this book. Below are books that will give you even more in-depth ideas about getting your work done.

More books on using to-do lists:

Getting Things Done: The Art of Stress-Free Productivity – David Allen

15 Secrets Successful People Know About Time Management – Kevin Druse.

Productivity for Creative People: How to get Creative Work Done in an "Always On" World – Mark McGuiness.

The Daily Entrepreneur: 33 Success Habits for Small Business Owners, Freelancers, and Aspiring 9 to 5 Escape Artists – S.J. Scott and Rebecca Livermore.

Manage Your Day to Day: Build Your Routine, Find Your Focus, and Sharpen Your Creative Mind – Jocelyn K. Glei & 99U Book Series.

Chapter 11: It's The Goal That Is Important

Daily Inbox Zero: 9 Proven Steps to Eliminate Email Overload (Productive Habits Book 5) – S.J. Scott.

How to get things done with One Note – Dominic Wolfe.

Level Up Your Day: How to Maximize the 6 Essential Areas of Your Daily Routine – S.J. Scott and Rebecca Livermore.

Websites and posts

"The Eisenhower Decision Matrix: How to Distinguish Between Urgent and Important Tasks and Make Real Progress in Your Life" – Brett & Kate McKay **www.artofmanliness.com/2013/10/23/eisenhower-decision-matrix/**

"Evernote to Nozbe Integration – Setup and Use – Taskclone" **http://support.taskclone.com/article/57-evernote-to-nozbe-integration-setup-and-use**

"How to Make a Moleskine PDA" – Brett McKay **www.artofmanliness.com/2009/04/27/how-to-make-a-moleskine-pda/**

"27 Ways to Get More Sh!t Done" – Laura Schwecherl **http://greatist.com/happiness/27-ways-get-more-sht-done**

"How to be Prolific: Guidelines For Getting It Done"

– Joss Whedon
www.fastcompany.com/1683167/how-to-be-prolific-guidelines-for-getting-it-done-from-joss-whedon

"Getting Things Done for Writers" – Angela Booth **www.angelabooth.biz/2010/10/getting-things-done-for-writers-new-series.html**

"The Rule of 3: Take Control of Your Day, Take Charge of Your Life" – Tony Khuon **http://agilelifestyle.net/the-rule-of-**3

"Scrivener and Evernote – A Perfect Pair" – Steve Shipley **http://steveshoutsout.blogspot.com/2013/10/scrivener-and-evernote-perfect-pair.html**

"Digitizing Literacy: Reflections on the Haptics of Writing | InTechOpen" – Anne Mangen and Jean-Luc Velay **www.intechopen.com/books/advances-in-haptics/digitizing-literacy-reflections-on-the-haptics-of-writing**

"The Emergent Task Planner" – Dave Seah **http://davidseah.com/node/the-emergent-task-planner/**

"Becoming an Email Ninja and Staying at Inbox Zero" – Danny Holtschke **www.slideshare.net/Danhol8/becoming-an-email-ninja-and-staying-at-inbox-zero**

APPENDICES

Appendix 1: Creating Email Folders And Filters

Filtering your emails increases your efficiency by allowing you to spend time on the communications that will have the greatest impact on your business. Feel free to modify the system described below to best fit the way you work.

First, create folders to store your major categories of email. An example set of folders would be:

- Newsletters
- Action Items
- Webinars
- To Read
- To File

How to create a folder

I will use Apple Mail as an example of how to set up folders and then discuss the use of Smart Folders. However, I also include a link to an online article on how to create folders in Gmail, Yahoo, and Outlook.

Apple Mail: Folders are called "Mailboxes" in Apple Mail.

1) At the top menu click on Mailbox

2) Go down to "New Mailbox"

3) You will see a dialog box with "On My Mac"

4) If you already have created mailboxes, you will see an up and down arrow; if you click on the arrows you will see all of the mailboxes you have created under each email address you have on your computer.

5) Select the where you want your mailbox and name your mailbox.

Smart Mailboxes

You can set up a smart mailbox for easy access to messages stored in other mailboxes. A really useful smart mailbox is a "Today" smart box. When you set up a Today smart box, you can specify that the mailbox will only display messages that were received today.

When you take the mid-day and evening check of your emails, you can quickly go through your Today smart box and apply your Do under 2 minutes, Defer, Delegate or Delete strategy. This is a great way to empty your Inbox on a daily basis.

Edit Smart Mailboxes

You can also Edit a Smart Mailbox and include additional criteria to your original criteria. For example, I set up a Smart Mailbox for any emails I flag during the day for my

Deferred emails. However, once I started using this smart mailbox, I realized I wanted to include any emails I received that were flagged for my attention or listed as priority 1. I opened Edit Smart Mailbox, opened my Flagged Smart Mailbox and clicked on the plus sign. I added an additional criteria: "Message has flag" Now I get both types of emails displayed.

Suggested Smart Mailboxes you might set up:

• Today

• Flagged

• Contains attachment

• Newsletters

You can learn more about Smart Mailboxes at

https://support.apple.com/guide/mail/use-smart-mailboxes-mlhlp1190/mac

Other mail programs

Mail for Windows: bit.ly/2o3hfU9

Gmail: https://support.google.com/mail/answer/118708?co=GENIE.Platform%3DDesktop&hl=en

Gmail uses labels rather than folders. The latest version also allows you to turn on or off the following tabs: "Primary; Social; Promotions; Updates; Forums."

Yahoo: www.lifewire.com/create-folders-to-organize-yahoo-1174476

Outlook: https://support.office.com/en-us/article/create-a-folder-in-outlook-3d3120d4-3c0e-4fef-b396-89b68324eba6

Using filters

Once you have set up your folders and Smart Folders in Apple Mail, you can create filters to specify that emails with specific subjects or from specific senders can go automatically to specific folders. There are a wide range of options for how to use these filters.

For example, I set up all the emails from dash@meetedgar.com, which is MeetEdgar's newsletter, to go to a folder titled, "Newsletters." I read these when I have time, but otherwise, don't have my Inbox cluttered up with newsletters.

How to set up a filter in Apple Mail

Go to "Mail" and click to display the drop-down menu.

Click on "Preferences."

1) Click on "Rules" at the far right of the top menu.
2) Click on "Add Rule" located on the right under "Rules."
3) Give your rule a name.
4) Choose where you want the email to go from a list of available mailboxes. For example, move email from admin@sistersincrime.org to a name "SINC Newsletter" mailbox.

How to set up a filter in Google mail

Open Gmail.

1) In the search box at the top, click the Down arrow.

2) Enter your search criteria.

3) At the bottom of the search window, click "Create filter with this search."

4) Choose what you'd like the filter to do.

5) Click "Create filter."

How to set up a filer in Microsoft Outlook

Click the "File" tab.

1) Click "Manage Rules & Alerts."

2) In the Rules and Alerts dialog box, from the E-mail Rules tab, click "New Rule."

3) Click on "Step 1: Select a template."

Appendix 2: Labels/Tags Used By Writers

Here are some common writer labels/tags to get you started. You can use several labels for a single file. For example, my label for the print version of Completing The Writer's To-Do List is:

Work Completed, print, 2018, BBFW

This combination of labels tells me:

The file is for the print version of a completed book in the Business Books For Writers series, written in 2018.

You can use whatever keywords you want for your labeling system, just document the labels you use and use them consistently.

Caution: Put thought into your labeling system. If you create the labels "Print" and "Printed" and use them interchangeably, you will need to do a search for both to find all the print files related to a specific work.

The Good News: You can always go back and change the labels on a file, add more labels to a file, delete labels, etc., so if you find that you have created a system that needs refinement, you can improve it. For maximum efficiency, just realize you will need to go back and make the change to all the files using your previous system.

Tip For Those New To Using Labels: Start out with broad labels and as you get used to using them, add more labels to your system. This will keep the labeling system cleaner and result in less need to back and change any type of redundancy as described with the print label example.

Below you will find some sample labels, followed by brackets with the sub-labels you might want to use:

General
[Year]

Work in Progress
[novel]
[short story]
[essay]
[non-fiction]

Work Completed
[published]
[unpublished]

Research

Expenses
[Administrative]
[Marketing]
[Advertising]

[Travel]
[Meals]
[Professional, Legal, Fees]

Co-authored work

Short Stories
[genre]
[year published]

Unpublished

Additional Resources

The *Completing The Writer's To-Do List* web page, **www.businessbooksforwriters.com/completing-the-writers-todo-list**, contains additional resources for readers of the Business Book for Writers series, including:

- General information of interest to writing entrepreneurs
- A list of corrections made after initial publication
- Download links for various templates of interest to writers and indie-publishers

Access the Resources page at:

www.BusinessBooksforWriters.com/Resources

Feedback from readers is always appreciated. If you have a resource to add to the page, or if you have discovered an error in one of the series books, please email Tonya Price: TPrice at TonyaPrice.com and the information will be added to the list so other writers (including Tonya) can benefit from your suggestion(s).

A Word From The Author

Thank you for purchasing *Completing the Writer's To-Do List*. I would love to hear how this book helped you to gain control of your to-do list rather than have your to-do list control you.

I especially want to thank those who also bought *The Writer's Business Plan* or *Meeting the Writer's Deadline*. Your loyalty and feedback contribute a great deal toward the continual improvement of the Business Books for Writer's series.

If you found the advice, tips, and information included in the book valuable, please tell others. Reviews help spread the word to other authors that there is a resource to help them avoid the stress that comes with an out-of-control to-do list.

Your feedback is always valued and incorporated into future editions of the book. Please send any comments, questions, and suggestion to

Email: TPrice at TonyaPrice.com.

Twitter: @BusBooks4Writer

LinkedIn: www.LinkedIn.com/in/TonyaDPrice

Facebook: www.facebook.com/BusinessBooksforWriters

Instagram: www.instagram.com/tonyadprice/

Pinterest: www.pinterest.com/busbooks4writer/books-on-the-business-of-writing/

Author site: www.TonyaDPrice.com

If you would like to continue to get helpful information, business advice, and information on contests, giveaways, and requests to participate in our beta reader program, please sign up for *The Writing Entrepreneur* **newsletter**. You can preview a copy of the newsletter on the signup page:

www.BusinessBooksForWriters.com/TheWritingEntrepreneur

The Business Books For Writers Series

Writers must juggle many tasks, so each book in this series was written to be read in a weekend. That is why none of the books exceed 30,000 words.

Most business books written for writers take a very broad look at publishing, marketing, etc. You learn a little about many topics in these books.

The Business Books for Writers series takes a different approach. Each book focuses tightly on a particular business topic that builds on previous books (although you can read them in any order and still get a great deal out of information from the books). For example, other business books may tell writers how to start a writing business and mention that you need a business plan. They do not provide step-by-step instructions for *how* to write the business plan, *why* you want to define your company's mission and vision statements, and *how* they are the foundation of your marketing, financial, and strategic plan. Rather than writing a business plan you create and never use, *The Writer's Business Plan* provides worksheets, templates, and examples to teach you how to write a business plan that will guide your success over your writing career.

The series also tackles business topics critical to achieving business goals, but not covered by other books. *Meeting the Writer's Deadline* illustrates how to meet your writing deadlines and stay on your book's schedule and budget. The book shows how to establish a writing schedule, rather than have a long list of uncompleted tasks. Once authors find themselves in control of their time and free from worrying about missing their deadline, they discover their creativity escalates, and they enjoy writing even more.

Over time, the Business Books for Writers series will expand. Our goal is to build a comprehensive library of books that will introduce writers the business skills they need to establish a successful writing career and business.

Tonya D. Price – Author of *Business Books For Writers*

Tonya Price has published short stories across a variety of genres and is the author of the Business Books for Writers series.

Tonya has an MBA from Cornell University and worked over 15 years in the high tech industry at the executive level. She is a serial entrepreneur working on her third venture as the founder of the indie publishing company, Magnolia Lane Press. One of the biggest challenges she faced as a VP and Director while raising two daughters was how to control a lengthy to-do list. Several hundred incoming emails a day threatened to sabotage her ability to get work done on a daily basis.

Completing the Writer's To-Do List details the process Tonya developed to manage the many tasks she faces as a writer. Throughout the *Business Books for Writers* series, Tonya always emphasizes the need for each author to customize her recommendations to what works best for them.

It is Tonya's sincere hope that with the lessons, techniques, and tips included in this book, you, too, will be able to go to bed each night knowing you have completed the work you needed to do for the day. It makes getting a good night's sleep much easier.

Available From Business Books For Writers

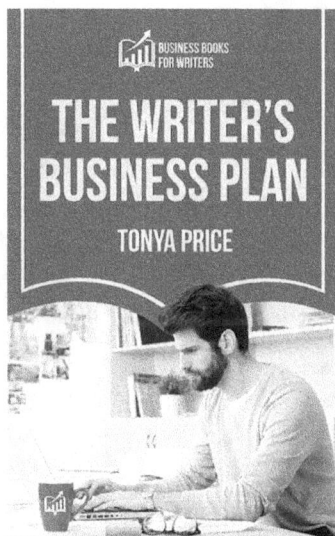

The Writer's Business Plan

The Writer's Business Plan gives you the knowledge to succeed — not with one book, but across your entire writing career. Written in clear language without jargon, *The Writer's Business Plan* guides you through creating your business plan in 7 simple steps. Save time with eleven downloadable worksheets and a business plan template.

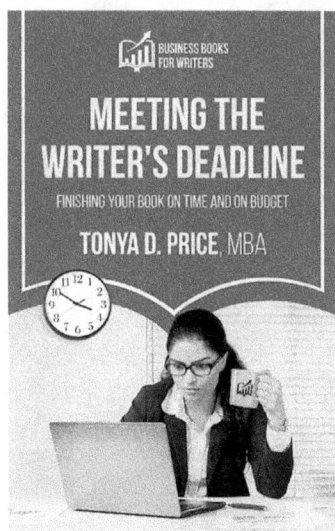

Meeting The Writer's Deadline

Spend a weekend with *Meeting the Writer's Deadlines* and learn the techniques and strategies you need to launch your book on time and on budget. Loaded with examples and tips to become a writing entrepreneur who reaps the benefits of meeting your deadlines.

Notes

Want easy access to the online links while reading? Go to

www.businessbooksforwriters.com/ctwtdl-links

[1] "The Pen is Mightier Than The Keyboard – Advantages of Longhand Over Laptop Note Taking," Pam A. Mueller, and Daniel M. Oppenheimer, Volume: 25 issue: 6, page(s): 1159-1168, Article first published online: April 23, 2014; Issue published: June 1, 2014.

[2] David Allen, *Getting Things Done, The Art of Stress-Free Productivity*, Penguin Books; Revised edition, March 17, 2015.

[3] Ibid.

[4] Tonya D. Price, *Meeting the Writer's Deadline*, Magnolia Lane Press, 2017.

[5] Steven Covey, *The 7 Habits of Highly Effective People,* Simon & Schuster; Anniversary edition, November 19, 2013.

[6] David Allen.

[7] J. D. Meier's book, *Getting Results the Agile Way*, October 18, 2011.

[8] Tonya D. Price.

[9] Psychologist World, "The Zeigarnik Effect Explained,"

Last checked 1/31/18. Original paper: Zeigarnik, B. (1927). "Über das Behalten von erledigten und uneredigten Handlungen," Psychologische Forschung. 9. 1-85. https://www.psychologistworld.com/memory/zeigarnik-effect-interruptions-memory

[10] Nick Hacker, "Using Scrivener and Evernote to Write Your Book," WriteHacked,

http://www.writehacked.com/writing/using-scrivener-and-evernote-to-write-your-book/ Last viewed: January 31, 2018.

[11] James Clear, "How Long Does It Actually Take to Form a New Habit? (Backed by Science)," http://www.huffingtonpost.com/james-clear/forming-new-habits_b_5104807.html Last viewed January 31, 2018.

[12] Zoe B., "8 ways to Reduce Distractions,"

https://simplelifestrategies.com/sls-reduce-distraction Last viewed July 24, 2012

[13] Brigid Schulte, "In two weeks, I went from 23,768 e-mails in my inbox to zero. Here's how," Washington Post online article, August 12, 2014, http://wapo.st/2H2Qnvf Last viewed January 31, 2018.

[14] Teresa Amabile and Steven Kramer, *What motivates you to work hard? The Progress Principle: Using Small Wins to Ignite Joy, Engagement, and Creativity at Work*, Harvard Business Review Press; 1 edition (July 19, 2011).

[15] Josh Specter, "Screw Your To-Do List. You Need A Done List," Medium.com. Jul 5, 2016 https://medium.com/an-idea-for-you/screw-your-to-do-list-you-need-a-done-list-ede0b82c748 Last viewed January 31, 2018.

[16] Leo Widrith, Lifehack, "Why To-Do Lists Don't Work and Done Lists Do," http://www.lifehack.org/articles/productivity/why-to-do-lists-dont-work-and-done-lists-do.html Last viewed January 31, 2018.

[17] Damon Zahariades, *To-Do List Formula: Stress-Free Guide to Creating To-Do Lists That Work*, CreateSpace Independent Publishing Platform. October 13, 2016.

www.ingramcontent.com/pod-product-compliance
Lightning Source LLC
Chambersburg PA
CBHW060857280326
41934CB00007B/1086